handmade
HOUSEPLANTS

REMARKABLY REALISTIC PLANTS YOU CAN MAKE WITH PAPER

CORRIE BETH HOGG

FOREWORD BY DAVID STARK
PHOTOGRAPHS BY CHRISTINE HAN

Timber Press • Portland, Oregon

Frontispiece: Fishbone cactus (page 138)

Published in 2018 by Timber Press, Inc.

The Haseltine Building

133 S.W. Second Avenue, Suite 450

Portland, Oregon 97204-3527

timberpress.com

Printed in China

Text design by Anne Kenady Smith

Cover design by Anne Kenady Smith and Hillary Caudle

Library of Congress Cataloging-in-Publication Data

Names: Hogg, Corrie Beth, author. | Han, Christine, photographer.
Title: Handmade houseplants: remarkably realistic plants you can
    make with paper / Corrie Beth Hogg; foreword by David Stark;
    photographs by Christine Han.
Description: Portland, Oregon: Timber Press, [2018] | Includes
    bibliographical references and index.
Identifiers: LCCN 2018000779 | ISBN 9781604698190
Subjects: LCSH: Paper flowers. | House plants.
Classification: LCC TT892 .H64 2018 | DDC 745.594/3—dc23 LC
    record available at https://lccn.loc.gov/2018000779

A catalog record for this book is also available from the British Library.

for: Cheryl, Mae
and Virginia

Contents

THE PAPER PLANTS

BONUS PROJECTS

FOREWORD

The kinds of artists who are shamans have always transfixed me. They make magic out of thin air. Their art looks untouched by human hands. It's as if the work just appears from the sky—never labored over. It just *is*.

Corrie Beth Hogg is one of those artists. For fourteen years, I have had the pleasure of collaborating with her under the auspices of my company, David Stark Design and Production. Over those years, our team invented many things that on paper might sound crazy, but brought to life were beautiful, often outlandish, full of whimsy, and made with the utmost attention to craft—so much so that even the wackiest idea was ultimately chic. Whether transforming the Grand Ballroom of the Waldorf Astoria hotel with a suspended canopy of tropical paper foliage for a Carnegie Hall jungle-themed gala or, swinging in the opposite direction of scale, creating intricate flowers and bumblebees from the pages of recycled books that live within the intimate confines of glass cloches, Corrie creates magic by transforming the everyday into the extraordinary.

How does she do it? Of course, it's hard to pin down exactly where an artist's golden touch comes from, but one of the things that I have always marveled at is Corrie's ability to break down process and create a system that provides a logical, methodical path to the desired outcome. I suppose it's a learned skill that came out of necessity. The events we produce at my company are often on a grand scale—for sometimes thousands of people; making every element of these environments and centerpieces would be impossible for one person to manage single-handedly.

Corrie, over the years, has become an expert at creating beautifully lucid, step-by-step instructions that empower each of our talented elves in the studio to create their own magic. It's so exciting for me to see how Corrie has honed those skills to create this book, packed with such generosity, tips and tricks, her own brand of quirky humor, and, most importantly, *great* ideas.

For those of us who love nature as well as the handmade, this charming book, filled with gorgeous photos, will become a favorite in our library. I suggest you use it not only as a fine tutorial to create your own version of Corrie's brilliant botanical garden, but also as inspiration. Do you line up five plush paper rex begonias interspersed with shimmering candles to beautifully appoint your Thanksgiving table? Do you create a window box for an inside ledge with your own garden of combined paper plants? There are thirty projects here to explore and perfect, but Mother Nature has waved her magic wand at many more species to explore on this earth. Take the methods that Corrie has so abundantly shared and apply them to your own favorite specimens or invent your own breed! And don't forget to have a good time. Corrie infuses fun and whimsy into everything she touches. Beyond her extraordinary artistic talents, I am lucky enough to be swept onto the fun train she conducts daily. That energy is infectious and is felt throughout this delightful book. You are in for a treat!

DAVID STARK
*author and president and chief creative officer of
David Stark Design and Production, a world-renowned
event design, planning, and production company*

Introduction

My love for nature and my passion for making art are intrinsically intertwined—and they always have been. As a child growing up near the Gulf Islands National Seashore in southern Mississippi, I spent many afternoons canoeing in the bayous and wandering trails in the woods. I'd construct giant dream catchers by pulling up ivy from our garden, twisting the vines together, and adding whatever treasures I found that day: feathers, shells, or acorn caps. I started art lessons at just eight years old, planning my artistic future at a young age. They led me to study painting at Memphis College of Art, before I moved to New York City to follow my *art world* dreams.

Although I love urban life, I took a break from the city a few years ago to work for a season on an organic farm in northern California. My tent dwelling allowed me to wake with the dawn each morning, and my days orbited around plants. I picked basil in the morning, weeded arugula after lunch, and patiently waited for tomatoes to ripen day after day. My favorite moments were once again merging nature and art together by creating mixed floral bouquets for the farmers' market and arranging the farm stand's vegetables in an appealing way.

I brought that state of mind back with me to Brooklyn, where I currently live and work just a few blocks from the Brooklyn Botanic Garden and Prospect Park, both of which I visit nearly every weekend. These outdoor spaces are invaluable to me for inspiration, fresh air, and a much-needed respite from city life. They're also where I discovered many of the plants that you'll find in this book.

Nature fuels and inspires me . . . whether that means backpacking the Appalachian Trail, taking a stroll in a park, or even just finding some small corner of my apartment where a few houseplants can survive. I began making paper plants because I wanted a fiddle-leaf fig tree in my windowless living room. From their verdant hues to their whimsical gestures, these paper creations give me the same joy as my live plants. Though the paper is temporary, especially when compared to a plastic plant, I believe the care and attention I put into each leaf while creating the plant makes me appreciate it even more.

Paper wasn't always my medium of choice. For many years, I made paintings, collages, and fabric sculptures. I began working with paper at the request of my longtime mentor and friend, David Stark, who wrote the foreword for this book. David's always known and trusted that I was a person who could make things. Even if I didn't know how, he knew I'd figure it out. I've worked at his company, David Stark Design and Production, for many years, and it's become my second home. My job gives me endless opportunities to be ambitiously creative, and I never know what I'll be inspired to make from one day to the next. This exciting variety at work gives me freedom to discover new ideas in my own studio, sparking inspiration—like my current obsession, paper plants!

A fiddle-leaf fig—the plant that started my paper plant-making career!

From my very first paper challenge of building a life-size baby giraffe out of kraft paper, to all the variations of flowers, birds, butterflies, and more, paper found its way into my heart and my own studio. I love to revel in the wonders of taking the ordinary, like paper, wire, and a bit of paint, to create an object that I truly cherish. As you craft your own versions of the projects in this book, I hope you start (or continue) your artistic journey in this manner. Celebrate the pure pleasure in the act of creating something new with your hands. Not every leaf needs to be perfect, not every cut or mark needs to be made exactly the same. Enjoy the process! Enjoy making these plants for yourself, for your home, or as a gift for a friend.

In this book you will find detailed instructions for making thirty of my favorite plants, plus five bonus projects demonstrating how to showcase the plants in artful ways. Many of these plants will probably be familiar, while some may seem more exotic. I chose *Pilea peperomioides* and fiddle-leaf figs because they are popular, and also because the real plants are difficult to come by or hard to take care of. Sometimes, I chose to make a plant simply because I love the color or the shape of the leaves. No matter the reason or inspiration, the great news is that paper plants don't require you to have a green thumb or a sunlit home. They simply require a set of willing hands, a few crafting supplies, and a good pair of sharp scissors!

Many projects in this book are easy and can be done in an afternoon, but a few may take a weekend to make. In most of the projects I've tried to closely mimic the real plant. But whether your muse is a realistic version or something cut from your own imagination, let yourself experiment and play. After all, creation at its core is whatever inspires, intrigues, or compels you. Are you ready to craft your own indoor garden? Let's make some paper plants!

Crafting baby leaves for the Never-Never Plant project.

Getting Started

Tools & Materials

In this chapter I'll cover my favorite tools and materials to use when making paper plants. They're easily found at art-supply and craft shops, and at any number of online vendors (I've listed a few of my go-to retailers in the Resources section). After you've familiarized yourself with all the necessary supplies, move on to the skills and techniques, in the next chapter, where you'll put these tools and materials to work.

TOOLS

Creating paper plants doesn't require a lot of special tools; in fact, you may already own many of the items listed here. Take the time to become familiar with my recommendations and check that what you have is in good shape—when you're cutting paper, nothing is more frustrating than a dull pair of scissors. Not every project in this book requires each of the tools listed below, but having the right tool for the job will help your projects come together smoothly and make your plant look as polished as possible.

BASIC TOOLS

METAL RULER AND SOFT MEASURING TAPE
You'll need a metal ruler to use as a straight edge when cutting paper with an X-Acto knife. An 18-inch [46-cm] (or longer) ruler is ideal for the projects in this book. You'll also need a soft measuring tape to measure the inside of your pots.

WIRE CUTTERS AND NEEDLE-NOSE PLIERS
You'll use the wire cutters for nearly every project in this book. The needle-nose pliers are essential for only a few.

MARKING UTENSILS You'll need a white pencil for tracing templates on dark paper (white lines are easier to see on dark paper), a No. 2 pencil, and a marker. It is also useful to have a pencil sharpener and good eraser on hand.

BONE FOLDER Typically used to flatten a crease when folding paper; use the pointed tip of this tool to press paper securely around the contours of the wires.

CUTTING MAT I recommend choosing a cutting mat that measures at least 16 × 22 inches [41 × 56 cm].

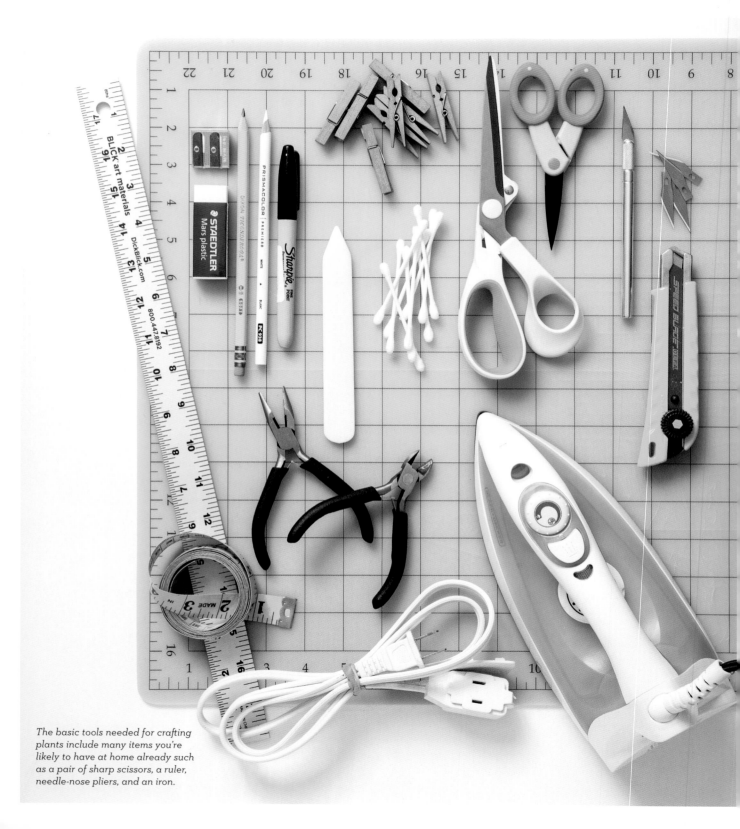

The basic tools needed for crafting plants include many items you're likely to have at home already such as a pair of sharp scissors, a ruler, needle-nose pliers, and an iron.

CLOTHESPINS A handy tool to have to hold glued pieces together while the glue dries.

COTTON SWABS These are useful for applying glue and alcohol.

SCISSORS Buy a good-quality pair of sharp and comfortable scissors. Designate them as your paper-crafting scissors and don't use them for fabrics or other materials (they'll dull faster). It is also useful to have a smaller pair of scissors for detail work, but this is not essential.

CRAFT KNIVES An X-Acto knife will help you make detailed cuts, and a utility knife is great for cutting thicker materials. Keep a supply of spare blades for the X-Acto knife on hand.

IRON An iron is my secret weapon in paper crafting. I recommend getting an inexpensive one to use exclusively for crafting. You can, of course, use an iron you already own, but be prepared to clean it after using it for some of these projects.

EXTENSION CORD An extension cord is not essential, but if your crafting table is far from an outlet, you'll be glad to have it.

Painting and mark-making supplies range from small paintbrushes to a spray bottle.

PAINTING TOOLS

PAINTBRUSHES I recommend having an assortment of soft-bristle paintbrushes on hand, including 1-inch [2.5-cm] flat brushes for washes, small flat brushes for applying glue, and small round and liner brushes for detailed work. Inexpensive chip brushes are also useful for dry-brush work and for applying gesso.

SMALL SPRAY BOTTLES These are useful for applying a thin splatter of watered-down paint or a gradation of color.

LARGE SPRAY BOTTLE Get the type with an adjustable tip—it's ideal for wetting paper evenly.

TOOTHBRUSH An alternative to small spray bottles for adding splatter to paper. Also, a toothbrush is a useful tool for cleaning your paintbrushes and spray bottles.

PALETTES For mixing and diluting paints. Find these at an art-supply store, or raid your recycling bin—empty yogurt containers are great for mixing paints.

BASIC WOODWORKING TOOLS

A couple of projects in this book require some woodworking implements. There is no need for you to be a skilled carpenter, but taking the time to get comfortable with these tools will help you step up your crafting game.

HANDSAW A coping saw is well-suited to cutting dowels to make tree branches, but other small handsaws will work, too. The coping saw pictured opposite is affordable, lightweight, and suitable for our purposes.

CLIPPERS Not typically listed among woodworking supplies, a pair of sharp clippers works well to cut small dowels to the size you need.

CLAMPS I prefer quick-grip-style bar clamps, but any medium-size clamps will work for the projects in this book. I recommend having at least two on hand. Clamps are essential for working safely; when they're paired with wood blocks they keep dowels from rotating while you're sawing them.

WOOD BLOCKS/WOOD STRIPS These are essential for using in tandem with clamps to keep round dowels stationary while you're sawing them.

DRILL/DRIVER A small cordless drill is ideal for the projects in this book.

DRILL BITS I recommend getting an assortment of drill bits ranging in size from $1/16$ inch [1.5 mm] to $1/2$ inch [12 mm]. They are typically sold in sets containing four or more sizes. Make a note of what sizes you have so that when you purchase dowels, you are getting the sizes that match.

SAFETY GOGGLES It's highly recommended that you wear protective eye gear when using a drill.

DUST MASK If you opt to work with Oasis foam, wearing a dust mask is essential.

Basic woodworking tools will come in handy for making tree-size paper plants.

Different types of paper are used for making leaves and flowers as well as for covering up wire connections on the underside of leaves.

MATERIALS

Choosing the right materials for your projects is important. I advise buying minimal quantities at first as you discover what works best for you and what brands you like. Most of the materials I use in this book can be purchased online, but I suggest that you visit your local art-supply store to handle these items in person to get a sense of how they look and feel.

PAPER

The majority of the projects in this book use either text-weight or cover-weight paper sized at 8½ × 11 inches [21.5 × 28 cm]. Text-weight paper is typically 28 to 36 lb. [12 to 16 kg]. Text-weight paper is easy to fold and manipulate, but it is not quite as thin as the paper you may see in a standard copy machine. Cover-weight paper, or cardstock, can be anything from 80 lb. up to 170 lb. [36 to 77 kg]. For the projects here, 80 to 100 lb. [36 to 45 kg] is ideal. Avoid using the construction paper you would typically buy for kids' projects; the quality is low and the color will fade quickly over time. Craft stores typically carry a variety of high-quality papers; they can also be found online. A few of my favorite suppliers are listed in the Resources section.

KRAFT PAPER A roll of kraft paper is useful to have on hand for testing leaf shapes and paints, for protecting surfaces you're working on, and for a few decorative applications described in this book. The color is a good match for the brown hues that are found in nature. Brown-paper shopping bags are a suitable alternative to kraft paper.

TISSUE PAPER A few projects in this book utilize tissue paper. I like to keep several green shades of it on hand to match the text-weight or cover-weight paper I am working with.

TRACING PAPER It's not essential for making the projects in this book, but tracing paper is useful for tracing the leaf templates provided at the end of this book.

CHIPBOARD Often found as packing material in a package of paper, this dense cardboard is perfect for making templates that can stand up to repeated use. Chipboard can also be purchased by the sheet at most art-supply stores.

OVERSIZE PAPER Two of the projects in this book have large leaves that require oversize paper. I recommend a cardstock or cover-weight paper at least 18 × 24 inches [46 × 61 cm] or larger.

*Floral tape and wire come in many colors,
perfect for crafting a garden of paper plants.*

FLORAL TAPE & WIRE

FLORAL TAPE Also known as corsage tape or stem wrap, floral tape is a slightly sticky, flexible tape available in a variety of colors and in widths of 1/2 inch [12 mm] or 1 inch [2.5 cm]. You'll need green, dark green, pink, red, black, brown, and orange for the projects in this book.

STRAIGHT FLORAL WIRE Straight floral wire (or stem wire) is typically available in 16-inch [41-cm] or 18-inch [46-cm] lengths. I prefer the paper-covered variety, available in red, green, black, or brown. Plain or cloth-covered wire will also work just fine. You'll need 16-, 18-, and 20-gauge wire for the projects in this book.

SPOOL WIRE Wire on a spool is typically thin and flexible. I use 24-gauge spool wire for the projects in this book.

ARMATURE WIRE This is a pliable wire that is typically used to make a structural frame for sculptures, but it's also great for making thick or long stems for paper plants. Armature wire is measured by its diameter rather than by gauge. The projects in this book call for 1/8-inch [3-mm] and 3/16-inch [5-mm] armature wire.

OASIS WIRE This is a 26-gauge wire covered with brown kraft paper. It's useful because its color resembles the brown hue found in plants and it's easy to manipulate. Oasis wire is very thin, however, so it's not suitable for large plants or plants that stand upright.

ADHESIVES

IRON-ON ADHESIVE "Ultra-hold" iron-on adhesive, typically used with an iron for appliqué techniques and fabric crafting, can be used with paper as well.

DOUBLE-SIDED ADHESIVE SHEETS Not all brands of double-sided adhesive sheets are created equal—some are just not strong enough. I prefer Grafix brand.

PASTE GLUE This adhesive comes in two forms: in a stick or as a thick liquid paste. Either type works for our purposes, and they can be used interchangeably.

WHITE GLUE I prefer the quick-dry, PVA, or acid-free varieties.

HOT-GLUE GUN AND GLUE STICKS I recommend a glue gun with a high-low switch. Setting the glue gun to "high" will make a stronger bond between the items you're gluing together. Hot-glue sticks come in two widths, so be sure to purchase the size that matches your gun.

MASKING TAPE AND PAPER TAPE You'll use classic masking tape to secure foam in pots, and you'll use brown paper tape to adhere wire to paper for one of the projects in this book.

Basic paste glue, a glue gun, brown paper tape, and adhesive sheets secure the wire stems and leaves together.

PAINTS & MARKERS

I use two types of paint in this book—acrylics and gouache. They have different uses and applications because of their inherent properties. Markers and gel pens also come in handy for adding fine details to leaves. Some projects will use two or more of these paints and pens to create the desired effect or pattern. All of the paints and markers below come in a broad spectrum of colors.

ACRYLIC PAINTS Acrylic paints are useful for painting large areas. You can dilute acrylics with water to add washes to paper, either with a brush or with a spray bottle. I also use acrylic paints when working with papier-mâché. Once acrylic paint has dried, it cannot be reconstituted.

GOUACHE PAINTS Gouache is an opaque matte watercolor paint. I use gouache paint to add details to a leaf after it's been constructed.

GEL PENS Opaque gel pens are available in a variety of colors and are excellent for adding thin decorative lines to leaves. I prefer Gelly Roll pens.

ALCOHOL MARKERS These are great for adding details to leaves with a lot of control. The ink bleeds into the paper for a natural look.

ALCOHOL Isopropyl alcohol, the kind found in a first-aid kit, can be used with alcohol markers to bleed decorative marks.

Acrylic paints, gouache, and gel pens are part of the plant-painting toolbox.

PAPIER-MÂCHÉ SUPPLIES

The projects in this book that require wood-working tools also require a few papier-mâché materials. There is no need to pick up anything fancy here, since you probably already have these supplies in your pantry.

FLOUR Although you can purchase a papier-mâché paste, good old-fashioned white flour mixed with water works just as well.

NEWSPAPER Raid your recycling bin.

BOWL AND WHISK You'll need a small mixing bowl and a whisk to make papier-mâché paste.

GESSO This is the artist's version of primer. An acrylic-based primer from the hardware or paint store also works.

SUPPLIES FOR LARGER CRAFTED PLANTS

PLASTIC TUBING Flexible, hollow, and available in different sizes at any hardware store.

DOWELS Wooden dowels are used for making trees. You'll need a variety of sizes, from 1/8 inch [3 mm] in diameter to 1 inch [2.5 cm] in diameter.

SKEWERS Regular wooden skewers (the kind used in cooking) are great for holding pieces of foam together.

BRICKS A large crafted plant can easily become top heavy and tip over. You'll want to counter this by adding a brick (or half a brick) to the bottom of your vessel.

Most of the supplies for papier-mâché can be found in your kitchen.

Plastic tubing, wooden dowels, and skewers are put to work when making larger plants. Bricks help stabilize a large plant or tree.

FOAMS

Foam is essential when it's time to assemble your plant in a pot—it holds the stems of the plant securely in place. There are many varieties of foam available for purchase. I have my favorites, but any of the foams listed below will work. Get thrifty: you can use the foam that large electronics are often packed in—you just need to cut it to fit your pot.

OASIS FOAM Oasis foam is a staple for many floral designers. This foam is the easiest to carve and shape, but it creates a lot of dust when it's being cut, so be sure to wear a dust mask to protect yourself. Oasis is well-suited for supporting smaller plants in pots.

STYROFOAM SHEETS AND FORMS Classic Styrofoam is available in sheets (you will need to cut them down to fit in your vessel) or round disks. They are easy to use when assembling your plant, but they can crumble with overuse.

INSULATION FOAM BOARD Typically used in home construction and found at big-box hardware stores, insulation foam is a dense and strong foam. Although this material requires more elbow grease than the others to cut it, I prefer it for its durability.

Foam is used for supporting stems in a vessel.

VESSELS

Here's an opportunity to get creative. You can assemble your paper plant in just about anything: classic terra-cotta pots, ceramic bowls, baskets, buckets, and more. Unlike living plants that need a watertight container, there are no restrictions for paper plants. Plant your creation in a decorative paper bag, a coffee mug, or a vintage pitcher. Don't be afraid to be a little playful and to think outside of the box . . . or pot!

Vessels are another opportunity to style your plant—they range from basic terra-cotta pots to textural baskets.

GROUND COVER

Once you have assembled your paper plant in a vessel, you will need to cover the foam. Many different materials will work. Most often, I use gravel, but shredded paper, moss, shells, larger rocks, or sand are also suitable. If you don't want to purchase a large heavy bag of gravel from a garden center, craft-supply stores often sell small bags of decorative rocks in the floral-design department, or you can find lightweight bags of pebbles in the aquatic section of a pet-supply store.

A PLACE TO WORK

I recommend setting aside space to work, whether it's a small table in the corner of your bedroom, or an entire room in your home devoted to crafting. Even if you're just using your dining-room table for the weekend, you'll need to get organized, gather all your tools and supplies, and protect your work surface. Being prepared at the onset is essential to seeing a project through to fruition. Set yourself up to succeed! Reserving space for making things will help ensure you can finish what you start. Even if you need to step away, your dedicated space is there, ready and waiting for you to jump back in. Pull up a comfortable chair, turn on some inspiring tunes, and get to work!

Various ground cover options.

My studio table is a dedicated space for crafting.

Skills & Techniques

I developed many of the skills and techniques that follow through trial and error, while other skills, like using floral tape, are commonly used by paper-flower artists. I've borrowed skills learned from my days as a painter and fabric sculptor and applied them to making realistic-looking paper plants. For example, painting paper with a lightly saturated brush allows you to add textural marks, while painting a diluted wash creates a more uniform hue. A few of these techniques may take a bit of practice to get the hang of, while others may come more easily to you. As you become more accomplished with these methods you can move on to developing your own repertoire of techniques.

PAPER PLANT PARTS

Before digging into the techniques for making leaf templates, painting details, and creating other paper plant elements, here's an introduction to the various parts of the plants featured in this book. Although many of the plants are vastly different once completed, the elements you'll craft to make them are all fairly similar.

LEAF The star of the show and the main element for every plant. Each cut-out paper shape is a leaf even when it has a blade or a fern shape.

LEAF STEM Once a wire is attached to a leaf, it becomes a stem.

SPRIG When a few leaf stems are connected together, they make a sprig. Sprigs make up the bulk of the plant shape.

VINE Similar to a sprig, but longer and trailing. When numerous leaf stems are connected together, they make a vine.

CROWN A thick and hardy stem at the base of the plant. It mimics the shape that protrudes from under the soil.

AERIAL ROOT An aerial root, also called a flying root, is a craggy linear growth that protrudes from a crown. Aerial roots are made with paper or floral tape and are nice styling details, enhancing the character of the plant.

BABY LEAF OR BUD Small leaves that are rolled to look like young leaf buds. They're used in a few plant projects to enhance the plant's realism.

FLOWER Only one project in this book calls for a flower to be made, and it's made of tissue paper.

MAKING & USING TEMPLATES

The first step for making every plant is creating a template. You'll find the template patterns for all the leaves in this book starting on page 252. You can either copy the templates from the book using a copy machine, or trace them onto tracing paper with a pencil. Most of the templates are life-size, but a few will need to be enlarged, as the size of the leaf is larger than the size of the pages in this book. The percentage a template needs to be enlarged by is noted on the page.

Cut out the copied or traced shape, place it on a sheet of chipboard, and trace around the leaf shape with a pencil. Carefully cut out the chipboard template with scissors and/or an X-Acto knife and label it with the plant name. Templates can be reused, so once you've finished making a plant, don't throw them away—save them to use again.

Some of the projects in this book require the leaves to be cut out before the wires are adhered to them, while others require the leaves to be cut out after the wires are adhered. Always refer to the tutorial before you start tracing and cutting leaves. When a leaf can be cut out before the wire is connected, you can use your template to fit as many shapes as possible on the sheet of paper; in those cases, the angle or direction of the leaf won't

Tracing a template.

matter. When leaves are cut out after the wire is applied, you'll need to line up the template with the wire, so the correct placement is essential. I like to keep on hand a No. 2 pencil and a white pencil for tracing templates. Since many of the papers I use to create plants are dark, I use the white pencil to trace around the templates—a white outline is easier to discern on dark paper.

ADDING COLOR TO PAPER

APPLYING WASHES & DRY-BRUSH TEXTURE

There are subtle shades of green in plant life that cannot be found in the colored paper available on the shelves of an art-supply store. Often, I choose paper in the closest hue and alter it by adding a thin wash of color using acrylic paint.

To make a wash, mix a small amount of paint with water in an approximate ratio of 1 part paint to $\frac{1}{2}$ part water. For example, if you're using 1 teaspoon [5 ml] of paint, dilute it with a $\frac{1}{2}$ teaspoon [2.5 ml] of water. You can easily create an even wash if you lightly mist the paper first with a spray bottle and water. This is called a "wet-on-wet" technique. The damp paper allows the diluted paint to be brushed on more uniformly without showing brush strokes. I also use this wet-on-wet technique when I want subtle color shifts and gradation with more than one shade of paint. When a second wash of diluted paint is applied to wet paper in small amounts, it bleeds and blends with the first wash. While the paint is still wet, you can spray another fine mist of water to further encourage the paint to flow.

To create textural marks, use a dry-brush technique with acrylic paint. A drier brush creates marks that are more scratchy and linear. For this technique, leave the paper dry and only minimally wet your brush by dipping it lightly in the paint so that just a few bristles are wet with paint. Then, paint the paper as directed in each tutorial.

The tutorials will tell you how many sheets of paper to prepare. Before you start cutting or gluing, I recommend that you paint as many sheets of paper as you will need first, then allow the sheets to dry fully before working with them. Dry the paper on a laundry-drying rack, or just spread them out on the floor on newsprint. If the paper is very wrinkled when dry, carefully flatten them out with a hot iron.

Top left: Using a spray bottle.
Top right: Painting a wash.
Bottom left: Painting paper with two colors.
Bottom right: Dry-brush technique.

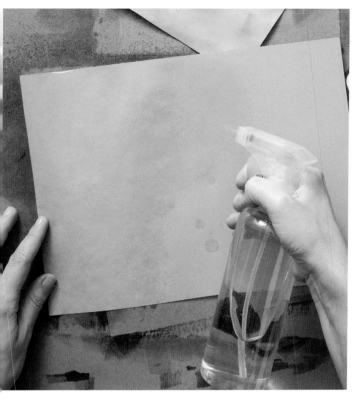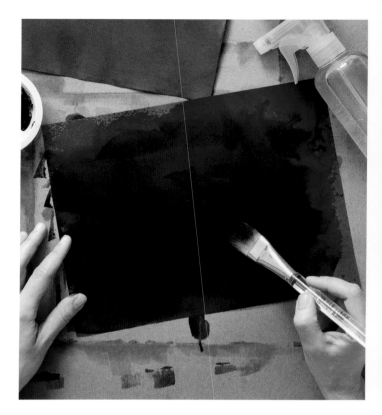

SPRAYING PAINT ON PAPER

Leaves in nature are often not a flat, uniform hue; they may be slightly speckled or textured. Replicating speckles and texture is fast and easy with a spray bottle, and it adds interest and realism to your paper plants. Start by diluting acrylic paint with water using a ratio of 1 part paint to 10 parts water and stirring it well. For example, if you use ½ teaspoon [2.5 ml] of paint, mix in five teaspoons [25 ml] of water. If you want a lighter shade, add a bit more water. Experiment with diluting acrylic paint to see what opacity you like—different colors may require more or less water. The easiest way to mix paint and water is in a dish or a clean yogurt container. Some brands of paint are more stubborn than others when you're diluting them and may require more stirring and mashing. When the paint is thoroughly mixed, transfer it to a spray bottle. I recommend using a small spray bottle with a cap so that you can use the paint again later, and so that the nozzle is protected from drying out with paint inside (it's a good idea to rinse out the nozzle when you're done using it, too). The distance you hold the spray bottle from the paper will vary the effect. For example, if you hold the bottle close to the paper, you'll get a concentrated mark and won't achieve an overall misted effect on the paper. And if you angle the bottle sharply,

Spraying paper with diluted paint.

you'll get more saturation closer to the spray bottle. I recommend experimenting with distance, angle, and amount of dilution. You can also apply different colors in layers for different effects. Prepare all the paper you need for a given project before you begin, and allow the sprayed paper to dry fully before you start working with it.

WORKING WITH ADHESIVES

One of the trickiest aspects of making paper plants is attaching paper to wire—it takes some practice to glue a flat object (paper) to a round object (wire). What follows are several methods that work for me. Some are interchangeable; others are not. As you make the plants in this book you may find that you prefer one technique over another, and once you gain experience you'll develop the skills to customize the projects to your taste and desired outcome. For instance, I prefer sandwiching a length of wire between two pieces of text-weight paper rather than attaching it to only one surface because it supports the leaf while still allowing it to be articulated and controlled, and it results in a more realistic-looking leaf. This approach also allows me to add decorative details to both sides of the leaf. This method, however, does not work for every leaf shape or plant type.

In some cases, I have chosen a specific adhesive because of the order in which different steps are taken to make a plant, or how the stem and leaf are joined—some leaves are perpendicular while others are parallel to the wire. Certain adhesives can take more abuse and manipulation than others. Hot glue, for example, is very strong but not very flexible. Iron-on adhesives are flexible but more time-consuming to apply. Double-sided adhesive sheets are quick, but you have to work with a sure hand, because this adhesive is permanent and cannot be repositioned. Paste glues are the most affordable, but they crumble and crack over time. White glues, although they dry clear and are somewhat flexible, may cause thinner papers to buckle from the moisture. I've found pros and cons to all the adhesives I've used, and each has its place in my toolbox.

PAPER TAPE METHOD

The quickest method for connecting wire to paper is using paper tape. This method is ideal for small leaves that are as narrow as the width of the tape, which is about 2 inches [5 cm]. Not all paper tapes are strong enough for this purpose, but the brown paper variety, typically used for sealing boxes, certainly is. Brown paper tape is also perfect for any plant that naturally has a brown underside or leaves that brown with age. When the brown tape peeks out from among a plant's leaves, it looks realistic. When you get the hang of this technique, keep it in mind for when you start inventing your own paper plants.

We'll use this method for the heartleaf philodendron, which in this tutorial has small leaves that are green on the top side and brown on the underside. You'll be positioning pairs of wires along the bottom and top edges of the paper and covering each pair with one piece of brown paper tape. With the sheet of paper placed horizontally in front of you, place a length of wire 1 inch [2.5 cm] in from the short end of the paper so that it overlaps the bottom edge of the paper by 1½ inches [4 cm] (or the correct distance for the leaf that you're making). Place another length of wire, also overlapping the paper by the same distance as the first, along the top edge of the paper.

Cut a length of paper tape to cover the two wires you just laid down, being careful not to move the position of the wire as you work, line it up with the edge of the paper, and tape the wires in place. Use a bone folder to press the tape around the contours of the wires. Repeat the above steps, placing the next wire 1 inch [2.5 cm] over from the edge of the tape you just put down. Keep going until you have eight wires attached with four pieces of tape.

HOT GLUE & TISSUE PAPER METHOD

Utilizing a hot-glue gun and paste glue, this method is ideal for hiding the connection where a stem protrudes perpendicularly from the leaf, but it can be used for other applications as well. This technique is used in four plant tutorials: *Pilea peperomioides*, watermelon peperomia, pitcher plant, and *Monstera deliciosa*. It can be used with both text-weight and cover-weight papers. In each case, you'll need tissue paper that matches the color of the leaf paper—the closer the color match, the better the illusion of realism. Please be careful when operating a hot-glue gun, because the metal tip and the glue itself can burn you (I have scars to prove it). Always unplug your glue gun immediately after use.

Start by tracing and cutting out your leaf shape. If a tutorial calls for the leaves to be sculpted into a three-dimensional shape, or for details to be added to the leaves, do that work first as directed in each tutorial. Next, using needle-nose pliers, bend one end of the wire to

Paper tape method.

make a small 1/8-inch [3-mm] loop (check each tutorial for the right gauge and length of wire). Once you've made the loop, grasp the loop with the pliers and bend it down so that it's perpendicular to the straight part of the wire. You've now created a surface—the loop—for the hot glue to adhere to. Apply a pea-size dot of hot glue to the back of the leaf shape and quickly place the wire loop into the glue. Hold it in place for several seconds as the glue hardens. Next, cut a 1-inch-diameter [2.5-cm] circle out of the matching tissue paper. Cut a slit from the

Making a loop.

Covering the connection with tissue paper.

edge of the circle to the center. (You can fold the tissue paper in order to cut several pieces at once.) Using a cotton swab or a small flat brush, generously apply a layer of paste glue to the tissue-paper circle. Holding the tissue paper where the slit is cut, place it around the wire, concealing the loop and the hot glue connection. Press and smooth the tissue paper.

PAPER STRIP METHOD

I use this method when I'm making a plant that has large but delicate leaves, and I want to preserve the thinness of the leaf paper. It calls for securing wire to a leaf by gluing paper strips over the wire. The paper strip holds the wire in place, but allows the rest of the leaf to be single ply. Projects that use this technique are the African mask plant, *Calathea orbifolia*, and white caladium.

Start by tracing and cutting out the leaf shapes as directed in each tutorial. Then, if the tutorial calls for it, apply decorative marks to the leaves and let them dry completely. Place a leaf facedown and line up a wire along the center of the leaf as directed by the tutorial. In some cases, the wire stem will protrude from the base of the leaf. In other cases, you'll want the wire to protrude from the center of the back of the leaf.

With the wire in place, apply a thin layer of white glue to a paper strip using a brush or cotton swab. Cover the wire with the paper strip, being sure to hold the wire in place. Press the paper strip down firmly. While the glue is still wet, press around the contours of the wire with the edge of a bone folder. Allow the glue to dry fully before attempting to bend or manipulate the wire.

IRON-ON ADHESIVE METHOD

Although it's the most time-consuming, this adhesive method has its perks—the adhesive can be dampened and will still stay adhered to the paper. I use iron-on adhesive when I want to wet a paper leaf to shape it. Yes, you read that right: wet a paper leaf! This is another reason why you want to avoid cheaply made paper—good-quality paper can stand up to abuse, including being painted, ironed, dampened, and painted again.

I use the strong, or ultra-hold, variety of iron-on adhesive, because it works the best with paper. Iron-on adhesive typically comes in a roll on a paper liner. The first thing I do is cut the roll down to 8½- × 11-inch [21.5- × 28-cm] sheets so it can be easily used with paper of that size. Instead of using an ironing board, I cover my worktable with an old terry-cloth towel folded in half. When you're ironing paper, you'll need a sizeable flat surface. A towel is ideal, as it is large enough and can be laundered after use.

I have two irons in my house. One has steam, spray, and eighteen different settings, and could probably send a text message—I use that one for my clothes. The other is an inexpensive iron I picked up at the dollar store, and it's strictly for working with paper. The iron that you'll use for working with paper just needs to get hot; there's no need for any bells or whistles. Please use an iron carefully, and never leave a hot iron unattended. We'll use this technique for the angel wing begonia, Swiss cheese vine, rattlesnake plant, and arrowhead vine.

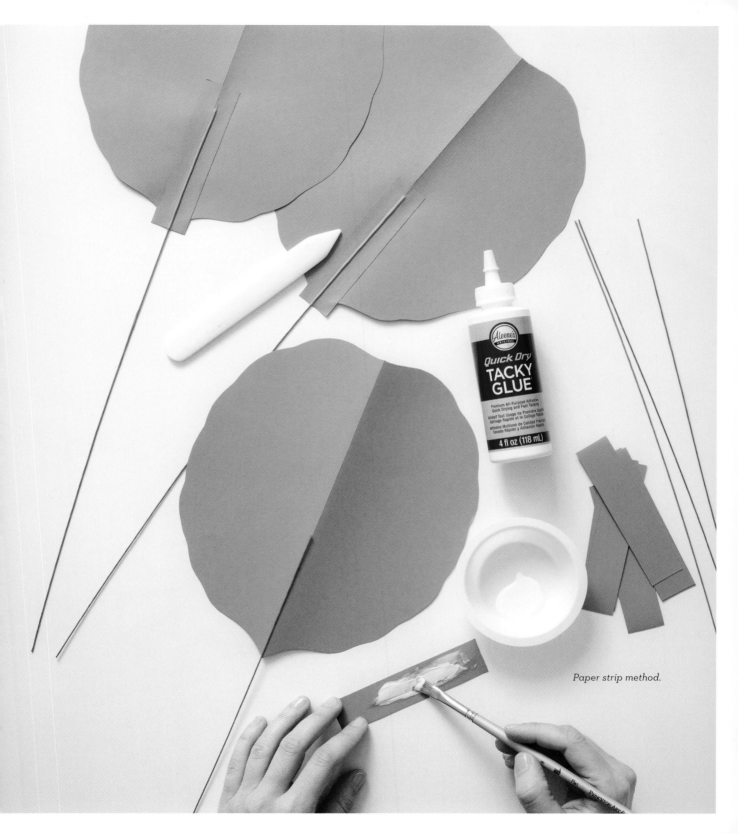

Paper strip method.

Iron-on adhesive method.

Half of the tutorials that use the iron-on adhesive method call for two different-colored papers to be used—a top color and a bottom color—to make a leaf that is one color on its top side and another color on its underside. All of them use text-weight paper and call for the wire to be adhered to the paper before the leaf shape is cut out. For this method, mock up the leaf templates on the paper and use a pencil to mark where to place the wires by making note of the base and center of each leaf, keeping in mind that the wire needs to extend into each leaf by at least 1 inch [2.5 cm]. Place a sheet of iron-on adhesive over the sheet of marked-up paper, lining up the edges of both sheets. The paper-liner side of the adhesive should be facing up, and the shiny adhesive side should be face down on the paper.

With the iron preheated on a hot setting (such as the cotton setting), iron the adhesive to the piece of paper by moving the iron over the whole page in two-second intervals until the entire surface has bonded. Allow the page to cool before handling it. Once cool, remove the paper liner. You should be able to see the pencil marks you made through the adhesive you applied, as it will now be clear. Using the pencil marks as a guide, position the wires. With the wires in their spots, place the second sheet of paper over the top, being sure to line up all the edges with the first sheet. Slowly iron over the paper-and-wire sandwich in eight-second intervals. Start gently at first, and as the wires start to feel like they are staying in place, use firmer pressure to press the paper around the contours of the wires. Tilt and use the hard edge of the iron to press the paper and adhesive around the contours of the wires. Repeat this on both sides of the paper, flipping over and working the contours of the wires for about eight seconds, and repeating on both sides until the wires are securely in place. Allow the paper to cool before handling.

DOUBLE-SIDED ADHESIVE SHEET METHOD

This is my favorite method, and the one I use most often in this book. It does, however, take some practice to align the pages, so I recommend practicing with scrap paper until you get the hang of it. Once you've adhered the pages together you cannot reposition them, so you need to be precise. Double-sided adhesive (also known as double-tack mounting film) is a thin layer of permanent adhesive protected on both sides by paper release liners. It's available in a variety of sizes. The first thing I do is cut each double-sided adhesive sheet down to 8½ × 11 inches [21.5 × 28 cm], so that it's ready to use. Save the excess—you can apply it instead of white glue when using the paper-strip method previously described.

Just as with the iron-on adhesive method, mock up the leaf templates on the paper and use a pencil to mark where to place the wires by making note of the base and center of each leaf and keeping in mind that the wire needs to extend into each leaf by at least 1 inch [2.5 cm]. For ease in aligning the paper and adhesive, position the leaf paper horizontally in front of you on a work surface. Remove the paper

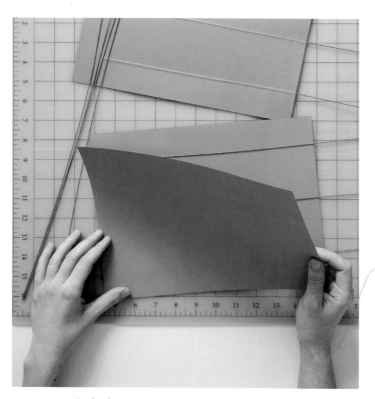

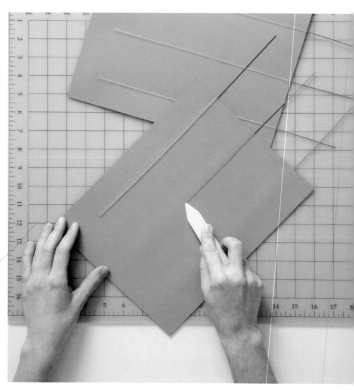

Make the paper and wire sandwich.

Press around the wire with a bone folder.

release liner from one side of the adhesive sheet. I like to hold the adhesive sheet horizontally, adhesive side down, with my hands positioned at either side of the sheet—my left hand is on the bottom left corner holding the edge of the adhesive loosely between two fingers, and my right hand is positioned in the middle of the right side. I hold my right hand closer to my body as I position the bottom left corner, aligning the adhesive sheet corner with the leaf paper corner, and only allowing that one corner to connect first. I slowly lower my right hand, allowing the adhesive to stick to the paper as it lays down, keeping everything in place with my left hand. Once the adhesive is applied, that's

it. There is no picking it up again and repositioning. I will say, and it happens to me, that if you accidentally get off alignment by ¹/₂ inch [12 mm] or so, it's not a loss. You can and should use most of the paper—just avoid that corner when positioning your templates and wire.

Now that the adhesive is in place, remove the second paper release liner and, using the pencil marks as a guide, press the wires onto the adhesive. Once the wires are in place, apply the cover sheet of leaf paper by aligning the lower left corners and using the same technique described above. Use your hands to gently press and smooth the paper down. Now that the wire is sandwiched between the two pieces of paper, use a bone folder to press the paper around the contours of the wires on both sides.

CUTTING OUT LEAVES

You can use either scissors or an X-Acto knife to cut out leaves, depending on what feels comfortable to you. In some tutorials, I have specified which cutting tool best suits a given leaf. Occasionally a tutorial will call for both tools, as an X-Acto knife tends to work better getting into tight spots or for cutting extreme curves, but scissors are often faster. When cutting out the leaf shapes made using the double-sided adhesive sheet method, the iron-on adhesive method, and the paper tape method, you will be faced with extra paper still adhered to the wire. Because adhesive has been used over the entire sheet of paper, the wire is adhered past the boundaries of the leaf shape. After you have cut out 99 percent of the shape, and you've gotten to the bottom where the wire connects, the best way to trim off the extra paper is to use an X-Acto knife to cut the paper over the wire on both sides. Next, cut a slit down the paper parallel to the wire inside. Fold back and pull the paper away. It should peel right off. Once you have cut out your leaf, check for any pencil marks and erase them.

ADDING DETAILS TO LEAVES

Adding details to the leaves enhances the plant's true-to-life appearance and gives them character. In some cases, the leaves are made from paper that has been treated with an acrylic wash of color. The reason I like to use acrylic paints when applying a wash is because when acrylic paint dries, it is permanent. Then, when I go back to add details with wet markers, pens, or paints, I don't have to worry about reconstituting any wash I have already applied and muddying up my color.

A combination of the methods, paints, and markers that follow may be needed to get a desired effect on a given plant. As you familiarize yourself with these techniques, you might find you prefer to work with markers over paints, or you may find that other combinations work best for you. That's all part of the fun!

Adding details with gouache paints.

GOUACHE PAINT DETAILS

Gouache paints are great for detailed work. I prefer to apply gouache paint last, as it can be smudged with water after it's dry. Gouache is always matte, which works well with paper.

The paint can be diluted with water to reach a desired translucency, or it can be used undiluted and remain completely opaque. For the projects in this book, a few drops of water in a pea-size dollop of paint should suffice to achieve the desired consistency. A little bit of gouache goes a long way. I recommend using soft-bristle brushes and a scrap piece of paper (the same color as the leaf you are working with) to practice making the marks and designs and to check if you are happy with the amount of translucency. For most of the projects, the painted detail should have the translucency of heavily fogged-up glass. The right tool for the job will help you succeed in making the desired mark; each tutorial will specify what size and type of paintbrush to use. Several of the projects in this book require that the leaves be painted with a specific pattern; the patterns for painting are on page 284.

Adding details with gel pens.

GEL PEN DETAILS

The favorite pen of teenagers across the globe is an excellent addition to your toolbox for drawing details on paper plants—the gel pen's thin lines are perfect for mimicking veins in leaves. The ink rolls on smoothly and opaquely, even on dark surfaces, and is available in a wide array of colors. Some projects combine gel pens with markers, others combine gel pens with gouache. Always replace the cap on your pen when you're finished, as these pens dry out quickly if left uncapped.

Adding details with alcohol markers and rubbing alcohol.

ALCOHOL MARKER DETAILS

Alcohol-based markers are artist-grade permanent markers that dry quickly in vibrant and saturated colors. Unlike water-based markers, alcohol markers are soluble only with alcohol. You can use a blending marker (an alcohol marker without pigment), or something more cost-effective: rubbing alcohol (isopropyl) and a cotton swab. Alcohol markers are available in a wide array of colors and tips.

If you want to use rubbing alcohol, start by pouring a small amount of alcohol in a small dish or cup. Replace the cap on the bottle, as rubbing alcohol evaporates quickly. As directed in each tutorial, draw the lines or shapes with the marker. Quickly dip the end of a cotton swab in the alcohol and rub it over the area of marker you'd like to bleed. More alcohol leads to more bleeding of the pigment. Allow each leaf to dry fully before handling. The alcohol and markers can bleed onto other surfaces, so be sure to protect your work surface with newsprint or scrap paper.

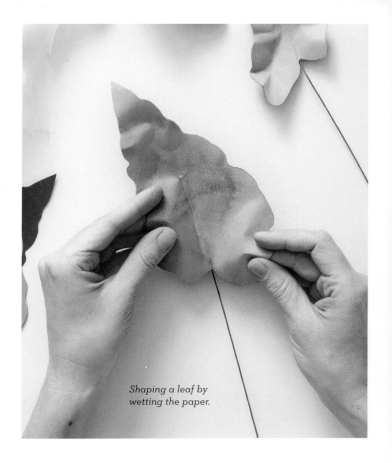

Shaping a leaf by wetting the paper.

WORKING WITH WET PAPER

One of the benefits of using iron-on adhesive to adhere wire to paper is that iron-on adhesive can stand to get wet. Iron-on adhesive is intended for use on fabric, which gets laundered, so it retains its adhesive equally well when dampened. I came up with this technique after watching a video of an origami artist mist his project with water in order to force the paper into a difficult thick fold. I had been trying to get my paper leaves to appear to be more undulating or wavy, and folding dry paper ruined this effect—the leaves were stiff and more hard-edged than I desired, or they simply did not hold the shape. Damp paper becomes malleable; unlike classic creasing, wet paper can be sculpted or shaped in two directions at once. This technique is useful when attempting to make small waves in thick paper, or for adding sculptural details to the leaves. Only use this technique on leaves that have been assembled using iron-on adhesive, since all the other adhesives used in this book will come apart when wet.

To use this technique, once you have cut out the leaf shape, lightly spray both sides of the leaf with a mist of water. Wait a couple seconds for the paper to absorb the water. Holding the leaf in both hands, pinch the paper between your fingers, working a little at a time, pinching and moving, varying the amount of paper you are manipulating. You may need to shape the wire inside the leaf at this stage as well. Add more water—just a light mist—if you need the paper to be more malleable. You can go too far, however: inexpensive papers will show wear more quickly, and all papers will pill and tear if overdampened or overworked. Once the leaf is shaped, set it aside to dry. It will dry in the shape you've molded it into.

ASSEMBLING YOUR PLANTS

WORKING WITH WIRE

Wire holds everything together in most of the projects in this book. Using the correct amount and gauge of wire called for in each project is important for the success and stability of your plants. For example, substituting a thinner gauge wire in place of a thicker wire can cause the finished plant to droop or tip over. This is particularly important for plants that stand upright; using the correct wire insures that they will stand on their own. You want your plants to be strong and sturdy, yet delicate and realistic, so the correct wire choice helps create this illusion.

Most floral wire is sold and labeled by gauge size; the smaller or thinner the wire, the higher the gauge number. The majority of the projects in this book use 16-gauge, 18-gauge, or 20-gauge straight floral wire; a few projects call for spool wire and armature wire. The good news is that it's very easy to add a supporting wire to your plant if you find it is starting to droop while you are constructing it.

WRAPPING WIRE WITH FLORAL TAPE

The first time you encounter floral tape, it is deceptive: it doesn't feel very sticky and it is seemingly thin and fragile. However, floral tape (or "stem wrap"), is a workhorse for many florists and paper-flower artists. Floral tape is essential, and we'll use it for nearly every project in this book. Floral tape is more like clay than tape, and it sticks well to itself and is very flexible. We'll use it to connect leaf stems together to create sprigs and vines, to change the color of a wire before we work with it, and to connect leaf stems to longer or thicker wires.

The adhesive in floral tape is released when the tape is stretched. To wrap wire with floral tape, start by lightly stretching a few inches of floral tape at the end of the roll. Take that end and pinch it around your wire. While pinching, turn the wire with one hand and pull the tape taut at an angle with the other hand. The goal is to have the tape completely cover the wire, overlapping just a little as you work down the length of the wire. To do this, it is essential that you hold the tape at a downward-slanting angle as you rotate the wire with your other hand. When taping two or more wires together, always make sure they are lining up straight and parallel, as bent wires will look odd through the tape. Always bend and shape stems *after* you have taped them. When you've taped the desired area, just give the tape a quick pull—it will tear and you can

Wrapping a wire stem with floral tape.

neatly wrap and press down the loose end onto your stem.

Don't be discouraged if it takes a little practice to master this technique! Working with floral tape becomes easier with time and repetition. I encourage you to practice by taping several wires before embarking on a project.

Preparing a vessel
with foam.

PREPARING A VESSEL WITH FOAM

As described in the materials section, you'll need foam to make your vessel ready for a paper plant. This is the method that works best for me, but there are other ways to assemble a plant in a pot, such as securing a plant's wire stems in plaster or cement; those approaches are more permanent, however. Here I've used 1-inch [2.5-cm] insulation foam, a soft measuring tape, a marker, a sharp utility knife, and masking tape. The foam needs to be at least 1 inch [2.5 cm] thick. Thicker foam is better—thin foam will not hold your plant in place.

To start, measure the diameter inside of the pot about ¾ inch [2 cm] from the top edge. Next, draw a circle on the foam with this measured diameter. If you don't have a compass, or if you need help drawing a circle, the easiest way to make a circle is to mark a center point on your foam and measure outwards. If the diameter is 6 inches [15 cm], measure 3 inches [7.5 cm] from the center in every direction, and make marks 3-inches [7.5 cm] out. Continue to measure 3 inches [7.5 cm] in different directions from the center point until you have enough marks and can complete the circle.

Carefully cut out the circle using a utility knife. Check the fit in the pot, and trim the foam if needed. If your pot tapers in, you will need to taper the edge of the foam. I do this by holding the knife at an angle and working my way around the circle of foam as I cut off a small wedge around the bottom. Check the fit again. If needed, repeat this process. Your foam should fit snugly in the pot, but it doesn't need to be perfectly shaped. Once the foam is wedged in place, cover any gaps along the edge of the foam with masking tape. The tape helps hold the foam in place and assists later when you cover the foam with gravel or sand by preventing it from shifting down to the bottom of the pot. If you are working with a straight-sided pot and you are finding it difficult to get the foam to fit snugly, pack the bottom of the pot with crumpled newspaper or another layer of foam before inserting the top layer of foam—either will support the foam at the desired height.

MAKING A CROWN

The bottom of a plant, just above where it goes under the soil, will often have what I call a "crown," or a thicker, hardier stem shape. Usually it is brown and woody in appearance. Several of the tutorials in this book call for this extra piece: the African mask plant, *Philodendron billietiae*, and *Monstera deliciosa*. To make a crown, you'll need foam, wooden skewers, white glue, a utility knife, a marker, brown kraft paper, clippers, brown acrylic or gouache paint, a paintbrush, a palette, and water.

To make a smaller crown, approximately 2 × 1 inch [5 × 2.5 cm], use a single layer of foam. For a larger crown, at about 2 × 5 inches [5 × 13 cm], stack and glue two pieces of foam together with white glue and set it aside to dry. Next, tear several long strips of kraft paper, each about 1 inch [2.5 cm] wide. Once the glue has dried, draw an arch shape on your foam with a

Carving the foam for the crown.

Inserting the crown into the foam in the pot.

marker and use your utility knife to cut it out. Work to carve the crown in three dimensions by rotating and cutting all sides and angles. When you are happy with the shape, wrap the foam crown with the strips of torn kraft paper, gluing them in place with white glue. Keep tearing bits of kraft paper, wrapping, and gluing until the miniature foam dome is covered. When the glue is dry, add areas of dark brown color with diluted brown paint. I like to add paint to the areas where the kraft paper overlaps. When the paint is dry, poke two or more wooden skewers into the bottom of the crown, making sure they are inserted straight up and down and parallel to each other. Use clippers to cut down the skewers until they protrude from the crown by about 2 inches [5 cm]. Holding the crown firmly, poke the skewers into the vessel prepared with foam, and press down until the bottom of the crown is flush with the foam. Later, when you're assembling the plant and inserting the stems into the crown, you should be able to poke through the layer of kraft paper into the foam. Ideally, your wires would be long enough that they can poke through the crown into the layer of foam in the vessel as well.

Inserting the wire stems into the crown.

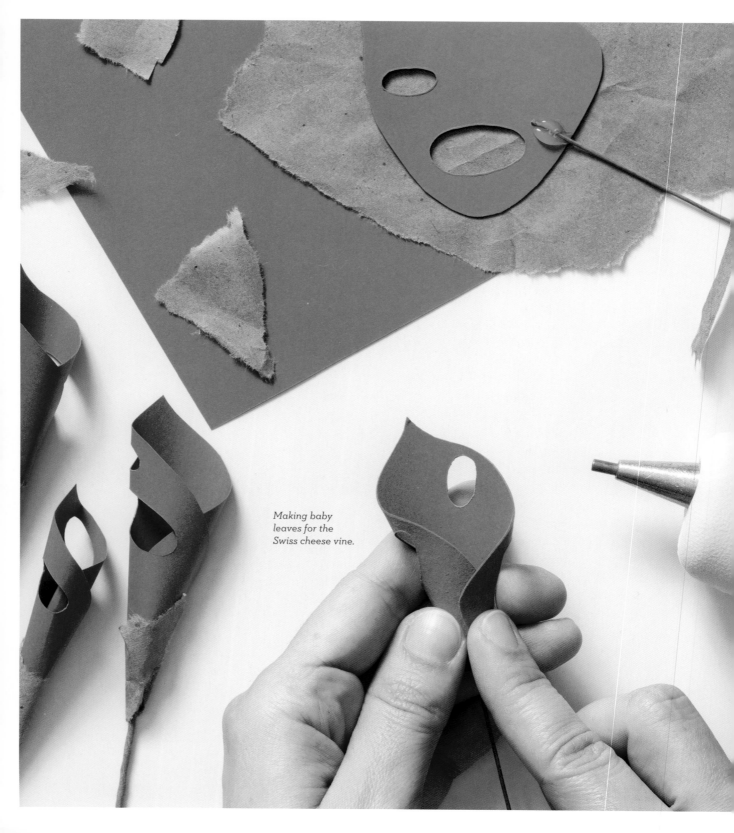

Making baby leaves for the Swiss cheese vine.

MAKING BABY LEAVES

To enhance the realism of my paper plants, I often add what I call a "baby leaf" or "bud" shape to the plant. I typically make baby leaves the same way, or a very similar way, for different plants; what varies is the color of the paper, the color of the floral tape, and the size of the baby leaf. You will find baby leaves on *Philodendron billietiae*, the Swiss cheese vine, and the never-never plant.

To make a baby leaf, start by cutting out a small leaf shape. I usually cut a small leaf shape freehand, because the leaf shape will be rolled and doesn't need to be cut perfectly. You can also use the top portion of a larger leaf for a baby leaf. Add a pea-size dot of hot glue to the center of the base of the leaf and quickly place the end of a straight floral wire into the hot glue. Hold it in place for a few seconds while the glue hardens. Roll the small leaf shape tightly by twisting the paper around the wire. Add a small dot of hot glue where the paper overlaps to secure the two edges together and hold the rolled shape. Cover the bottom of the baby leaf where it connects to the wire with floral tape and continue wrapping the rest of the wire. Shown here, the Swiss cheese vine calls for a piece of craft paper around the base of the baby leaf. Place these buds strategically so that they are visible after you arrange your plant.

PLANTING & STYLING

Part of the fun of making paper plants is choosing where they go. I once planted a paper plant in my friend's favorite mug from college. Planting is also what brings your paper leaves, vines, and stems to life. Arranging them thoughtfully is a good way to mimic the real thing. Before you begin constructing a plant, consider where it will be displayed. For example, you might arrange the vines to hang down from the right side of the pot, because you already know that you want to put the plant on the right side of your dresser and not the left. Maybe you have a dark corner in your living room that needs a pick-me-up, but you only have a narrow space; in a case like that, you'll want to construct a plant that's suitable for that spot and choose an appropriate vessel. Most of the plants in this book are intended to be planted in small or medium-size pots—about 2 to 10 inches [5 to 25.5 cm] in diameter. But, that does not mean plants can't be adapted to fit larger or smaller vessels.

The easiest way to insert a wire stem into the foam in your pot is to hold the wire an inch or two from the end and slowly press it down into the foam so that it penetrates the foam by 1 to 2 inches [2.5 to 5 cm]. Oasis and classic Styrofoam are easy to insert wires into; insulation foam may take a little more pressure. If you find you are having a hard time inserting the wire into the foam, it could be that the wire is soft, or too light a gauge; try using a heavier-gauge wire to poke a pilot hole in the foam before you insert the wire stem. Or, try holding the wire closer to the end; if you're holding the wire or stem too far from the end, the pressure you apply will bend the wire rather than insert it into the foam.

Style the leaves or vines of the plant before you insert them in the foam in the pot.

Finessing the leaves of the pilea.

Do this by grasping the leaf and wire with one hand and the supporting wire with the other hand. Gently pull down or twist the leaf to the desired location or angle. Try not to have each leaf line up in a row—adjust the angles slightly to create nuance, rhythm, and interest. Your eye on styling should not stop there. When you are arranging the plant in the pot, pay attention to its overall shape. I suggest looking at online images of the real plant to see how it drapes or stands. I like my paper plants to be visually balanced but not symmetrical; I don't want them to look like they are about to topple over, nor do I want them to look so perfectly positioned that they look fake. One of the tricks to making paper plants look realistic is to place the leaves as if they are leaning toward the light just like leaves on a live plant would, even if the window is in a galaxy far, far away.

Covering the foam.

COVERING THE FOAM

Some of the plants you make will be so dense and full that you won't need to worry about covering the foam—it simply won't be seen. Others, like the *Pilea peperomioides* or sassafras seedling, benefit from covering the foam, which helps to finish and finesse its appearance. Most of the time I prefer to work with small gravel, because I like the way it looks. I suggest adding the ground cover of your choice in small amounts, spreading it out evenly as you work. Don't mound or overfill your pot, as this will just be an annoyance later when you move it. Simply fill the space and add enough to completely cover the foam. Small pebbles or gravel are available in many colors, especially at pet-supply stores. You can find colors like hot pink, neon orange, white, tan, and black, in 5 lb. [2 kg] or 20 lb. [9 kg] bags. I prefer to use white, brown, or black gravel.

MAKING LARGER PLANTS

Larger paper plants are quite fun and rewarding to make. However, they require more time, more materials, and more space, both to create and to display. Don't let that deter you, though—a large paper plant makes an excellent addition to a small room. Just go vertically and place it on a small table or stool! I've had a large paper tree in my living room for more than four years and it is still standing! If made well, a paper plant can last and last. We will tackle three large plants in this book: *Monstera deliciosa*, fiddle-leaf fig, and tapioca plant. The fiddle-leaf and tapioca are made nearly the same way, differing only in the leaves and how the tree is painted.

WORKING WITH PLASTIC TUBING & WIRE

We'll use this plastic-tubing and armature-wire trick for only one project in this book, *Monstera deliciosa*. However, this technique is useful for any plant with thick hearty stems, so keep it in mind when you start "branching out" into other paper plant varieties. The basic principle of this technique is similar to the hot-glue and tissue-paper method previously described. You'll need a hot-glue gun and some glue sticks, 3/16-inch [5-mm] armature wire, 1/2-inch [12-mm] plastic tubing, monstera leaves that you've already cut out, matching tissue paper, scissors, wire cutter, needle-nose pliers, 1-inch [2.5-cm] dark green floral tape, and paste glue.

Just like when you're wrapping a wire with floral tape, cover a length of plastic tubing, making sure you are pulling the tape taut and overlapping it enough so that the tape sticks to itself as you work along the length of the tubing. Next, if the armature wire is coiled, do your best to straighten it out. Using needle-nose pliers, make a 1-inch [2.5-cm] loop at the end the armature wire. Then, grasp the loop with the needle-nose pliers and bend it so that it's perpendicular to the length of wire. With a hot-glue gun, squeeze a dime-size dot of hot glue on the back of the leaf. Quickly place the looped end of the armature wire into the dot of glue and hold it in place for several seconds while the hot glue hardens. When the glue is dry and hard, find something for the wire to lean against so that it can stay upright (if it falls over it may damage the paper leaf). Slip the plastic tubing over the length of wire until it meets up with the paper and hot-glue connection you just made. Cut three 2-inch [5-cm] doughnut-shaped pieces out of the matching tissue paper, and cut a slit on one side of each. Using a cotton swab or brush, apply a layer of paste glue to one of the doughnut-shaped tissue pieces, then wrap it around the base of the tube and hot-glue connection. Repeat this step until you have completely covered the connection and the base of the tube. Keep the tube with the wire inside propped up against something so that everything dries upright. Allow the glue to dry before moving the leaf and stem.

Top left: Wrapping a length of plastic tubing with floral tape.

Top right: Making a loop and attaching the armature wire.

Left: Covering the connection with tissue paper.

PREPARING A VESSEL FOR A LARGE PLANT

This method is similar to the method for adding foam to smaller vessels, so it should feel familiar to you, but there will be a few added steps. For larger pots, you'll need to insert two layers of foam. Because many of the larger plants or trees are top-heavy, securing the dowels and wires in thick doubled-up foam is essential for preventing the plant or tree from tipping over. If your vessel is lightweight, I recommend adding a brick or other heavy object to the bottom of the pot. If a brick is too large, add half a brick. (To easily and quickly break a brick in half, wrap it in an old towel and tap the middle of the brick firmly with a hammer; it should break in two.)

For the *Monstera deliciosa* project, measure the width of the pot at both ¾ inch [2 cm] and 1½ inches [4 cm] from the top edge with a soft measuring tape. Cut circles out of the foam at both of these dimensions and taper the edges of the foam if need be to match the pot. Secure the foam in the vessel with masking tape, starting with the smaller circle and stacking the larger one on top, wedging them in until they are snug. For the trees, measure the width of the pot about halfway down from the rim, but make sure to leave room for any brick or other object you've placed at the bottom. Take another measurement at about ¾ inch [2 cm] from the top edge. Cut each of these circles from your foam, and again, make sure to taper

the sides of the foam to better match the pot. Find the center of each circle and cut a 1-inch [2.5-cm] diameter hole directly in the center. Do this step carefully, making sure the hole in each piece of foam is centered and lined up with the other hole. You may need to use an X-Acto knife as well as a utility knife to make the holes. Place the smaller circle in the pot first, making sure it sits level and fits snugly. Use masking tape to secure it in place. Add the larger circle to the pot, pressing it down evenly to secure the foam. Cover any gaps along the edge of the foam with masking tape.

WORKING WITH DOWELS & PAPIER-MÂCHÉ

Wooden dowels are an excellent addition to paper crafting. They are found in nearly every art-supply and hardware store. They are inexpensive, easy to work with, and versatile. I always keep a stash of dowels in my studio, as they are useful for so many things. I feel the same way about papier-mâché! It's a technique typically used for Halloween masks and kids' science projects, but papier-mâché is an easy, unpretentious solution for many crafts.

USING DOWELS TO MAKE A TREE

We'll use the same techniques to make the basic tree shape for the tapioca plant and the fiddle-leaf fig. Gather the woodworking

*Preparing a vessel
for a tree.*

tools described on page 18. You'll also need an assortment of dowels in a variety of diameters. I used one 1-inch [2.5-cm], one 3/16-inch [5-mm], two 1/4-inch [6-mm], and two 5/16-inch [7-mm], each 48 inches [1.2 m] long, to make one tree. I recommend purchasing a few extras of each size, as the thinner dowels can break.

You've already prepared a vessel with foam with a 1-inch [2.5-cm] hole cut in the center. Thread the 1-inch [2.5-cm] dowel through the two holes as far as it will go, until it hits either the bottom of the pot or the brick. Check that you like the height it rises to from the surface of the foam. Each pot is different, so you will need to use your judgment, I typically like my trunk to stand about 30 to 40 inches [76 cm to 1 m] above the pot. The final height will depend upon where you intend to place the finished plant, how tall your pot is, and your personal taste. If you want the 1-inch [2.5-cm] trunk to be a bit shorter, mark the height with a pencil. Remove the dowel from the pot and place it on your worktable so that the cut mark is just past the end of the table and the longer portion of the dowel is on the table. About 6 inches [15 cm] from the mark you made, place a wooden block on each side of the dowel, each parallel with the other, and use a clamp to secure the blocks around the dowel. Next, use a second clamp to clamp the blocks (with the dowel wedged between them) securely to your work surface. You should not be sawing or drilling on your fancy dining-room table; I recommend using an old worktable, or a piece of plywood on a pair of sawhorses. Use a coping saw (or another kind of handsaw) to saw off the part of the dowel you'd like to remove. Apply gentle back-and-forth sawing motions with the coping saw. There's no need to force it—let the saw do your work for you. The cut doesn't need to be perfect, so don't worry if it isn't. (Cutting down dowels with smaller widths can easily be done with clippers.)

Once you have your trunk cut to the desired height, it's time to add a 6-inch [15-cm] length of a 1/4-inch [6-mm] diameter dowel to the end. To do this, leave your 1-inch [2.5-cm] dowel securely clamped to the work surface.

Before you work with a drill, familiarize yourself with a few safety precautions: wear protective eye gear, do not wear gloves, and be mindful of your clothes, hair, and jewelry, making sure that nothing is hanging loose and at risk of being caught in the drill. With a 1/8-inch [3-mm] bit inserted into your drill, drill a pilot hole in the center of the blunt end of the 1-inch (2.5-cm) dowel. Switch out the 1/8-inch [3-mm] bit for a 1/4-inch [6-mm] bit and drill a 1/2-inch [12-mm] deep hole to the end of the dowel. Insert the 1/4-inch [6-mm] dowel into the hole you just made. You may need to twist it to get a snug fit.

Now it's time to add branches. I typically add about 10 branches to each tree. Cut your dowels roughly in half, using your clippers. With your 1-inch [2.5-cm] dowel still clamped to the table, drill a small pilot hole, using a 1/8-inch [3-mm] bit, at about 4 inches [10 cm] from the end of the 1-inch [2.5-cm] dowel. Switch to a 3/16-inch [5-mm] bit, and as you drill in perpendicularly to the 1-inch [2.5-cm] dowel, slowly tilt the drill as you work to make a hole at a slight angle. You are tilting so that your hand and the drill are closer to the top of your tree. Don't drill all the way through the 1-inch [2.5-cm] dowel—a hole about ¹⁄₂ inch [12 mm] in depth will suffice. Unclamp the 1-inch [2.5-cm] dowel, rotate it by about a third, and clamp it again. Repeat the above steps slightly above or below from where you have just drilled. Unclamp and adjust the blocks and the clamps, rotating the 1-inch [2.5-cm] dowel again by a third and adding another hole. This time, use a ⁵⁄₁₆-inch [7-mm] bit after you've made a pilot hole. Unclamp and move the clamps down the length of the 1-inch [2.5-cm] dowel. Start another series of holes around the dowel about 4 to 6 inches [10 to 15 cm] away from the first set. Keep track of where you're creating the holes, and add them at slightly different positions around the dowel.

Ultimately, you will make ten holes: two ³⁄₁₆ inch [5 mm], four ¹⁄₄ inch [6 mm], and four ⁵⁄₁₆ inch [7 mm]. Work down the length of the dowel, adding two to three holes around the dowel every 4 to 6 inches [10 to 15 cm]. Always start with a pilot hole and then move up to the larger bit, and always clamp your 1-inch [2.5-cm] dowel securely to the work surface. If by accident you go all the way through the dowel, it's okay!

Once you have added ten holes at the various sizes, unclamp everything and reinsert the 1-inch [2.5-cm] dowel into your prepared pot. Match each hole with the correct dowel. Carefully insert the dowel into the corresponding hole. Hold the trunk with one hand, near where you are inserting the smaller dowel, and hold the branch with the other hand, close to the

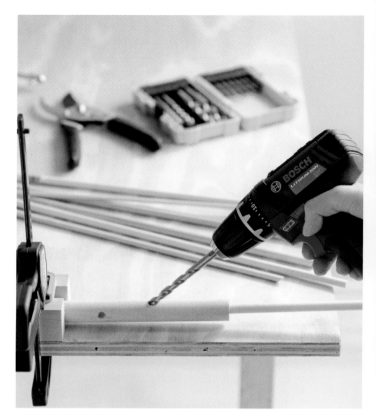

Drilling holes in your 1 inch [2.5 cm] dowel to add branches.

end you are inserting. You may find you need to twist the smaller dowel to get it in securely.

When you have inserted them all, stand back and assess the shape of your tree. With your clippers, trim the branches to create your desired overall shape. I trim my branches to lengths ranging from 16 to 24 inches [41 to 61 cm]. The reason I like to wait till I've constructed the whole tree before I cut down the dowels for the branches is because I like there to be variety in the lengths of branches—I want some to be shorter and some to be longer—yet I also want to maintain balance throughout the whole sculpture.

WORKING WITH PAPIER-MÂCHÉ

Now that your tree is constructed, it is time to papier-mâché it. Papier-mâché helps hold the branches and trunk together, and its inherent texture is what makes the dowels look like the bark of a tree. First, you'll want to smooth out the transition from the trunk dowel to the branch dowel at the top of the tree. You can do this by crumpling a small piece of dry newspaper and wrapping it around that juncture. Next, secure the piece of newspaper in place with masking tape. Wrap the tape around the paper, overlapping both the trunk dowel and the branch dowel, gripping and shaping the tape and paper until it forms a gradual slope. Next, tear about six pages of newspaper into 1-inch [2.5-cm] strips. Newspaper easily tears in the long direction (against the type). Then, tear the strips into lengths about 5 inches [13 cm] long.

Making papier-mâché paste is easily done with flour, water, a bowl, and a whisk. I recommend mixing a small amount to start and then making more as you need it. A one-to-one ratio is ideal for papier-mâché paste; this means ½ cup [125 ml] flour to ½ cup [125 ml] water, whisked together in a bowl. The paste should be about the consistency of pancake batter. Cover your work surface with a drop cloth or several layers of newspaper.

When working with the paste, you can wear gloves if you like. I prefer to just use my hands; even though it is messy, I feel like I have better control using bare hands. Dip one piece of torn newspaper into the papier-mâché paste, fully submerging it and covering both sides. With the strip in one hand, use two fingers of the other hand to squeeze down the strip's length, removing any excess paste. Apply the strip to the tree by wrapping it and pressing it down evenly along all the edges of the paper. I like to start at the bottom of the tree and work my way up. I suggest that you allow the strips to cover and secure the bottom of the trunk to the foam as well, as this will help stabilize the tree in the foam base. You'll want the strips to overlap each other a little, as you are aiming to completely cover the trunk and branches but without building more than one layer. Apply a single layer of papier-mâché strips over the entire tree.

Once the tree is covered, allow it to dry overnight. This step is important! You want the paste to be dry through and through, as any trapped moisture may mildew or rot over time. It is important not to trap that moisture! Once thoroughly dry, apply a second layer of papier-mâché to each juncture point: wherever you inserted a branch and where the tree connects to the foam. Allow the second layer to thoroughly dry as well. Clean up any papier-mâché paste that may have dripped onto your pot.

Covering the tree in papier-mâché.

GESSO & PAINT

I use gesso in many projects because it is a staple in my studio—I always have it around—but the acrylic or water-based primers available at any paint or hardware store will work just as well. Paint gesso or primer over the entire tree—everywhere that you've applied papier-mâché. This step is important, because it seals in the smell of the flour used in the papier-mâché, which can attract bugs or rodents. When the gesso is dry, follow the instructions in each tutorial for painting the tree with acrylic paints. It's important to fully cover the areas where you have used gesso. Acrylic paint is essential for this step; like gesso, it acts as a layer of sealant. When the paint is dry, follow the instructions in each tutorial on how to attach the leaves.

Painting the tree with gesso.

GIFT WRAPPING A PAPER PLANT

To gift wrap a paper plant, choose a shallow box that doesn't have sides that are high enough to press against the leaves of your plant, and place the plant in the center. Fill in the space around the plant with shredded paper or raffia. Write a message on a pretty gift tag and attach it to a ribbon wrapped around the box. Voila! Your handmade plant is ready to delight a friend or family member.

WHEN "OOPS!" HAPPENS

Mistakes and accidents happen! They're part of the art-making process. Even though I have been crafting for years and have made many paper plants, I still occasionally run into problems. I always try to see any stumble as a learning experience, figure out how to fix it, and move on. In this section, I will highlight common mishaps you might have and how to recover from them.

DEALING WITH DUST I recommend using a large, soft-bristle paintbrush or feather duster to carefully clean your paper plants. They will get dusty over time, and the darker-colored plants will show that dust more easily. Clean 'em up!

FADING FROM SUNLIGHT This too can happen, and unfortunately, it's hard to predict. Different papers use different qualities and quantities of pigments that may or may not react to sunlight. I had one plant start to fade, and I caught it before it was too far bleached. I found I didn't mind the subtle color shift of the leaves. Just be mindful from the outset: sunlight can bleach your paper plants!

DAMAGED LEAVES Your cat scratched it. You bumped into it. It was splashed with wine at your holiday party. Paper sculptures of any type are fragile, and that goes for paper plants as well. If a leaf is damaged, I recommend removing that vine or stem from the pot and unwrapping the floral tape (starting from the bottom), carefully setting aside each leaf until you reach the offending one. Remove that leaf and make another if you need it, then reassemble the vine or stem using the same color floral tape and reinsert the vine or stem into the pot.

HOT GLUE WON'T STICK I have heard this one before. The usual culprit is a low setting on the glue gun, or the glue gun itself is a low-temp glue gun. The bond made by a low-temp glue gun is not as secure as the one made using a hot-temp glue gun. It's so hot that you'll need to run for the sink if you accidentally touch the glue gun's tip or the molten glue. It could also be that you are not moving fast enough as you work. Hot glue hardens fairly quickly. Set all the pieces for a project in order before you start gluing, and keep everything within arm's reach so that you can quickly apply the pieces together.

A WIRE FALLS OUT Occasionally, a wire will fall out of the paper-and-wire sandwich. You are, after all, gluing a round object to a flat object. I find this happens most often with the iron-on adhesive method. It usually happens for one of two reasons. First, the bond was probably not made well to begin with. For the next time, remember that the iron-on adhesive is best activated within eight seconds while ironing around the contours of the wire. Second, the leaf might have been overworked while you were shaping it with water. The good news here is that both problems are easily fixed. Simply apply white craft glue to the end of the wire that goes inside the leaf, insert the wire back into the original channel, and hold it in place with two clothespins. Allow it to dry for ten minutes or so before removing the clothespins.

THE PAPER IS "PILLING" WHEN PAINTED This is due to either low-quality paper or overworking the paper with a paintbrush. When you're applying a wash, be confident with your strokes—don't overwork the paper by brushing too many times over in the same spot; it will damage the paper.

THE PAINT WON'T COME OUT OF THE SPRAY BOTTLE In all likelihood, the nozzle is clogged. Try soaking the nozzle in warm water and then cleaning it with an old toothbrush. You might also need to further dilute your paint.

As you work, remember to be patient and kind to yourself! You are learning and trying something new. These are good and admirable things! Enjoy the process and making the projects that follow. Post your work on social media—I'd love to see your paper plants! Tag your photos with #HandmadeHouseplantsBook.

The
Paper
Plants

Heartleaf Philodendron

The heartleaf philodendron, one of the first plants I endeavored to make from paper, appropriately gets its name from its charming heart-shaped leaves. This plant can be found in dark green, variegated, or lemon-lime color varieties. Also known as *Philodendron hederaceum*, the heartleaf has been cultivated as an indoor plant for hundreds of years. This beauty translates well into paper, especially with the chartreuse color we'll be using here. The young leaves of the lemon-lime are slightly brown in color, lending itself perfectly to our brown paper tape.

TOOLS

Scissors

Bone folder

Pencil

X-Acto knife

Wire cutters

MATERIALS

2 templates (page 262)

7 sheets of 8½- × 11-inch [21.5- × 28-cm] chartreuse text-weight paper

Brown Oasis wire

Brown paper tape

Five 16-inch [41-cm] lengths of 18-gauge brown straight floral wire

Brown floral tape

Vessel prepared with foam

Gravel or ground cover of your choice

Plant notes: This plant is composed of approximately 110 leaves in two sizes. It consists of 5 vines of various lengths with 10 to 12 leaves each and 10 sprigs with 5 leaves each in a 4-inch-diameter [10-cm] pot. The approximate finished size is 17 inches high x 13 inches wide [43 x 33 cm].

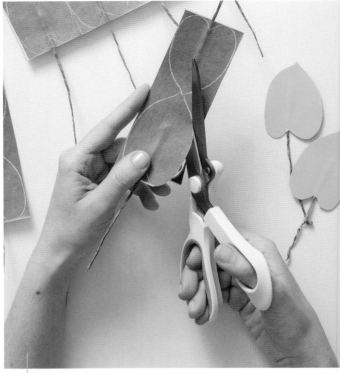

STEP 1

CONNECT THE WIRE AND PAPER.

Start by cutting the 8½- × 11-inch [21.5- × 28-cm] paper in half, so that you have 14 pieces of paper measuring 8½ × 5½ inches [28 × 14 cm]. Next, cut 110 pieces of brown Oasis wire to 6-inch [15-cm] lengths. Following the directions on page 39 for the paper tape method, secure the wires to the paper.

STEP 2

TRACE AND CUT OUT THE LEAVES.

Position the 2 templates over the wires in the paper-and-tape sandwiches, making sure the wires protrude from the crevice in the base (not the pointy end) of the leaf shapes, and trace approximately 55 each of the large and small leaf shapes. Using scissors, cut out the leaves. If necessary, use an X-Acto knife to carefully cut around the wire at the base of the leaf to release the paper that is adhered to the stem.

STEP 3

CONNECT THE STEMS TO MAKE VINES AND SPRIGS.

To make a vine, use wire cutters to cut a 13-inch [33-cm] length of Oasis wire. Starting with 2 smaller leaves, attach the stems to the end of the vine wire about 2 inches [5 cm] from the base of each leaf by twisting the leaf wires around the vine wire. Continue to twist leaf stems around the vine at approximately 1-inch [2.5-cm] intervals as you work down the length of the wire. Alternate randomly between attaching large and small leaves until you have attached approximately 12 leaves. Repeat these steps to create three 13-inch [33-cm] vines with approximately 12 leaves each, two 10-inch [25.5-cm] vines with 10 leaves each, and ten 6-inch [15-cm] sprigs with 5 leaves each.

STEP 4

CONNECT THE VINES AND SPRIGS TO 18-GAUGE WIRES.

Cut a 5-inch [13-cm] length of 18-gauge brown straight floral wire for each vine and sprig. Connect the 18-gauge wire to the end of each vine and sprig by twisting about 2 inches [5 cm] of the Oasis wire around the 18-gauge wire. Cover both with a layer of brown floral tape.

Starting with the longer vines first, assemble the plant by inserting them into the vessel prepared with foam. Fill in with the shorter sprigs to flesh out the shape. Cover the foam with ground cover.

Pilea peperomioides

Pilea peperomioides, or Chinese money plant, is one of my favorite plants to make. It has also been a favorite among the readers of my blog. *Pilea pepero-mioides* is a well-loved and admired plant, but if you've ever tried to acquire one, you've probably noticed that it's quite hard to come by. The pilea does not grow from seeds; it only propagates by sending off shoots from a healthy adult plant. These offshoots have been shared across the globe to the lucky few! More common in Europe, the pilea is hard to find elsewhere, which is why a paper version is terrific!

TOOLS

Pencil

Scissors

Container for glue

Clothespins

Wire cutters

Needle-nose pliers

Hot-glue gun and glue sticks

MATERIALS

3 templates (page 260)

2 sheets of 8½- × 11-inch [21.5- × 28-cm] dark green text-weight paper

Paste glue

Cotton swabs

Lime green gel pen

Ten 16-inch [41-cm] lengths of 20-gauge green straight floral wire

Dark green tissue paper

⅛-inch [3-mm] armature wire

Brown floral tape

Vessel prepared with foam

Gravel or ground cover of your choice

Plant notes: The draping specimen pictured here is composed of 25 leaves, and the 2 upright plants are made with 15 to 18 leaves each. Both are planted in 4½- to 6-inch [11.5- to 15-cm] high pots. The approximate finished size of each plant is 12 inches high x 9 inches wide [30.5 x 23 cm].

STEP 1

TRACE AND CUT OUT THE LEAVES.

Use the 3 templates to trace the leaf shapes onto the text-weight paper, or draw various sizes of circles freehand. Depending on how large you'd like your finished plant to be, trace or draw 15 to 25 leaf shapes. Use scissors to cut out the leaves.

STEP 2

ADD THREE-DIMENSIONAL SHAPE TO THE LEAVES.

Using scissors, cut a slit in a leaf from the edge of the circle to the center. Use a cotton swab to apply a thin line of paste glue along one edge of the slit. Pull the opposite edge of the slit to overlap the first, creating a shallow bowl shape. Press the edges together and use clothespins to hold the connection in place as it dries. Allow the glue to dry fully. Repeat for all the leaves.

STEP 3

ADD DETAILS TO THE LEAVES.

Using a lime green gel pen, make a small dot in the center of each leaf. The ink will stay wet for about a minute, so allow each leaf to dry before you handle it again.

STEP 4

CONNECT THE WIRE TO THE LEAVES.

I like to make the stems for each pilea leaf a slightly different length, as the variety adds to the realism of the plant. Using wire cutters, cut the 20-gauge wire to lengths ranging from 4 to 7 inches [10 to 18 cm] long, cutting enough wire to make one stem for each leaf. Next, prep the wires and adhere them to the point on the back of the leaves with hot glue by following the instructions on page 40 for the hot glue and tissue-paper method. Be sure to hold each wire in place for several seconds as the glue hardens.

STEP 5

COVER THE CONNECTION.

Cover the wire and hot-glue connection on each leaf with matching tissue paper by following the instructions on page 40 for the hot-glue and tissue-paper method.

STEP 6

CONNECT THE STEMS.

Reserve 2 or more leaves to stand alone in the pot. Using wire cutters, cut a 12- to 16-inch [30.5- to 41-cm] length of armature wire to create the main stem and straighten it out if it's coiled. Using brown floral tape, wrap the stems of 2 small leaves to the end of the main stem about 3 inches [7.5 cm] from the base of each leaf. Continue to wrap leaf stems 3 to 4 inches [7.5 to 10 cm] below the base of each leaf to the main stem at 1/2- to 1-inch [12-mm to 2.5-cm] intervals as you work down the length of the wire. Alternate randomly between attaching large and small leaves and turn the main stem as you work so you are adding leaves onto different sides. Attach as many leaves as you like and wrap the remainder of the armature wire with brown floral tape.

Starting at the bottom of the main stem, bend the leaf stems out to create the plant shape. Next, bend the main stem to create a gentle curve, or arch it to drape down the side of the pot. Insert the main stem into the vessel prepared with foam and further adjust the leaves to your liking. Insert the reserved leaves at the edge of the pot and cover the foam with ground cover.

Watermelon Peperomia

Peperomias are a large genus of plants, with more than a thousand identified species. They're popular houseplants. This variety, named for the watermelon-rind stripes on its leaves, which we'll create with gouache paint, is native to Brazil. You can make a lush plant, like I have here, or something more minimal with only a few stems. The medium-size leaves are so ornamental and beautiful all on their own—they even look great as a single stem in a bud vase!

TOOLS

Pencil

Scissors

Container for glue

Clothespins

Small round paintbrush

Palette

Wire cutters

Needle-nose pliers

Hot-glue gun and glue sticks

MATERIALS

Template (page 262)

6 sheets of 8½- × 11-inch [21.5- × 28-cm] dark green text-weight paper

Paste glue

Cotton swabs

White gouache paint

Eighteen 16-inch [41-cm] lengths of 20-gauge brown straight floral wire

Dark green tissue paper

Vessel prepared with foam

Gravel or ground cover of your choice (optional)

Plant notes: This plant is composed of approximately 36 leaves in a 3-inch-diameter [7.5-cm] pot. The approximate finished size is 8 inches high x 12 inches wide [20.5 x 30.5 cm].

STEP 1

TRACE AND CUT OUT THE LEAVES.

Use the template to trace the leaf shapes onto the paper, fitting as many as you can on each sheet (about 6 to 7 leaves per sheet). Trace approximately 36 leaf shapes, then use scissors to cut out the leaves.

STEP 2

ADD THREE-DIMENSIONAL SHAPE TO THE LEAVES.

Using scissors, make a 1-inch [2.5-cm] cut in each leaf from the base (the curved end, not the pointy end). Use a cotton swab to apply a thin line of paste glue along one edge of the slit. Pull the opposite edge of the slit to overlap the first, creating a shallow bowl shape. Press the edges together and use clothespins to hold the connection in place as it dries. Allow the glue to dry fully.

STEP 3

ADD DETAILS TO THE LEAVES.

Using white gouache paint lightly diluted with water, and a small round paintbrush, paint a dot in the center of each leaf. Next, paint watermelon-rind-style stripes extending from the dot to the edge of the leaf. Use the pattern for painting on page 286 as a guide, or paint each leaf freehand.

STEP 4

CONNECT THE WIRE TO THE LEAVES AND COVER THE CONNECTION.

Using wire cutters, cut the wire to 8-inch [20.5-cm] lengths, cutting enough wire to make 1 stem for each leaf. Next, prep a wire, adhere it to the back of a leaf, and cover the connection with matching tissue paper following the directions on page 40 for the hot-glue and tissue-paper method. Repeat for all the leaves.

I leave all the stems the same length to start, then I cut down a few stems as I assemble the plant to help give it a rounded shape. Bend the wires into slight curves to create the mounded plant shape. If the foam is visible, cover it with ground cover.

Pitcher Plant

Some biologists believe the pitcher plant evolved over millennia by the gradual rolling and folding of a leaf shape—the very same process we'll use to create this paper version. I am totally smitten with carnivorous plants! They often have unique color combinations, usually to attract insects, but they attract people and folklore myths, too. Widely depicted as menacing in popular culture, the pitcher plant is truly harmless and delightful. I've always wanted a live pitcher plant, but they can be quite difficult to care for. Thankfully, with the paper version, I don't have to worry about how much to water it—or finding flies for it to eat.

TOOLS

Containers for mixing paint

2 small spray bottles

Pencil

Scissors

Wire cutters

Hot-glue gun and glue sticks

MATERIALS

2 templates (page 253)

Pink and white acrylic paint

7 sheets of 8½- × 11-inch [21.5- × 28-cm] chartreuse text-weight paper

Three 16-inch [41-cm] lengths of 20-gauge green straight floral wire

Chartreuse tissue paper

Glue stick

Vessel prepared with foam

Gravel or ground cover of your choice

Plant notes: This plant is composed of 10 leaves, 4 large and 6 small in an 8-inch-diameter [20.5-cm] pot. The approximate finished size is 10 inches high × 10 inches wide [25.5 × 25.5 cm].

STEP 1

PREPARE THE PAPER.

Following the instructions on page 38 for adding color by spraying paint, fill a spray bottle with diluted pink acrylic paint, and fill another spray bottle with diluted white acrylic paint. Orient a sheet of paper horizontally and spray a mist of pink paint along the top edge of the paper. Once the pink paint is dry, lightly spray white paint over the pink and allow to dry fully. Repeat along the same edge on the back side of the paper, spraying pink and then white paint. Repeat on 2 more sheets of text-weight paper, for a total of 3 painted sheets. Next, orient another sheet of text-weight paper vertically and repeat the above steps to paint the top edge of the front and back of 4 sheets of paper. Allow the paper to dry fully.

STEP 2

TRACE AND CUT OUT THE LEAVES.

Use the large template to trace leaf shapes onto the paper you prepared vertically, with the painted edge at the top (the pointy end) of the template. Use the small template to trace the leaf shapes on the paper you prepared horizontally, also with the painted edge at the top of the template. Trace 4 large and 6 small leaf shapes. Use scissors to cut out the leaves.

STEP 3

CONNECT THE WIRE TO THE LEAVES AND COVER THE CONNECTION.

Using wire cutters, cut the wire to approximately 5-inch [13-cm] lengths, cutting enough wire to make 1 stem for each leaf. Next, adhere a wire to the center of a leaf with a line of hot glue. The wire should overlap the leaf from the base by about 3 inches [7.5 cm]. Using scissors, cut the matching tissue paper into ten 1- × 3-inch [2.5- × 7.5-cm] strips. Using a glue stick (or a cotton swab and paste glue), generously apply a layer of glue to a tissue-paper strip. Cover the wire with the tissue paper and smooth the tissue paper. Repeat for all the leaves and allow the glue to dry fully.

STEP 4

SHAPE THE LEAVES.

Fold a small crease in the center of the "head" portion of each leaf. Then, work to roll the paper into a tubular shape. You can gently press the paper over the edge of a table to aid in getting it to roll. Once you have achieved the shape, apply a line of paste glue along one edge and pull the opposite edge to overlap the first and press them together as the glue dries. Hold for a few more seconds as the glue dries fully. Repeat for each leaf.

Insert the wire stems into the vessel prepared with foam. Cover the foam with ground cover.

African Mask Plant

The African mask is a hybrid developed from plants that originated in tropical areas. The leaves are such a dark, rich green they can appear almost black. I love how graphic the two-toned leaves are, with their white veins and wavy edges. This plant makes for a striking and dramatic addition to any room. It's perfect in paper, as the real version is poisonous to cats or children or bunnies or whoever else may be eating houseplants at your house.

TOOLS

Palette

1-inch [2.5-cm] flat, ¼-inch [6-mm] flat, and a small round paintbrush

Scissors

Container for glue

Pencil

Bone folder

Wire cutters

Utility knife

Hot-glue gun and glue sticks

Large spray bottle with water

Clippers

MATERIALS

3 templates (pages 255, 256)

Black and brown acrylic paint

12 sheets of 8½- × 11-inch [21.5- × 28-cm] dark green text-weight paper

White and green gouache paints

Fifteen 16-inch [41-cm] lengths of 16-gauge green straight floral wire

White glue

Foam

Skewers

Kraft paper

Vessel prepared with foam

Gravel or ground cover of your choice

Plant notes: This plant is composed of approximately 15 leaves of various sizes and 2 crowns, all in a 7-inch-diameter [18-cm] basket. The approximate finished size is 20 inches high × 17 inches wide [51 × 43 cm].

STEP 1

PREPARE THE PAPER.

Following the instructions on page 36 for making a wash, paint a wash of black acrylic paint on both sides of each sheet of dark green paper. Allow the first side to dry fully before painting the other side.

STEP 2

TRACE AND CUT OUT THE LEAVES.

Reserve 1 sheet of paper for making strips. Use the 3 templates to trace approximately 7 large, 4 medium, and 4 small leaf shapes on the remaining sheets of paper. Use scissors to cut out the leaves.

STEP 3

ADD DETAILS TO THE LEAVES.

Mix green and white gouache paint to create a pale green color and lightly dilute the paint with water. Using the pattern for painting on page 285 as a guide, paint decorative lines on each leaf with a small round paintbrush, painting fewer lines on the small leaves.

STEP 4

CONNECT THE WIRES TO THE LEAVES AND COVER THE CONNECTION.

Cut the reserved sheet of painted paper into fifteen 1- × 4-inch [2.5- × 10-cm] strips. Place a large leaf pattern side down and position a 16-inch [41-cm] wire in the center of the leaf, overlapping the paper by about 4 inches [10 cm] with the remainder of the wire protruding from the center of the crevice of the leaf shape. Following the instructions on page 42 for the paper strip method, cover the wire with a paper strip. The strip should be positioned about ½ to 1 inch [12 mm to 2.5 cm] from the center of the crevice. Secure the wire in place by pressing the bone folder around the contours of the wire. Repeat for all the large leaves. Next, using wire cutters, cut 8 lengths of wire at 10 to 12 inches [25.5 to 30.5 cm] long. Repeat these steps to connect the wires to the medium and small leaves (you may need to trim the paper strip for the smaller leaves).

STEP 5

CREATE A CROWN.

Following the instructions on page 55 for making a crown, create two crowns for this plant, 1 small and 1 medium size. Insert the crowns into the vessel prepared with foam.

STEP 6

SHAPE THE STEMS.

In one hand, hold a leaf firmly where the wire is attached to the leaf. Bend the length of wire down with your other hand, arching the stem just above where it connects to the leaf. Repeat for all the leaves.

Insert the wire stems into the crown, poking the stems through the layer of kraft paper into the foam in the vessel. Arrange the leaves at different angles. Cover the foam with ground cover.

White Caladium

Typically planted outdoors and not often seen as a houseplant, the white caladium is a head turner! You won't find many leaves in nature that are as bright a white as the leaves of white caladiums. One of the items on my bucket list is visiting the caladium festival in Lake Placid, Florida, one July and touring the many fields of these beauties. What a sight that must be—row upon row of dazzling varieties, from hot pink to red to green, and speckled like splatterware. They must be just as stunning as the tulip fields in the Netherlands!

TOOLS

Pencil

Scissors

Containers for glue and isopropyl alcohol

¼-inch [6-mm] flat paintbrush for applying glue

Bone folder

Wire cutters

MATERIALS

2 templates (pages 268, 269)

14 sheets of 8½- × 11-inch [21.5- × 28-cm] white text-weight paper

Dark green alcohol marker

Cotton swabs

Isopropyl alcohol

Fifteen 16-inch [41-cm] lengths of 16-gauge green straight floral wire

White glue

Vessel prepared with foam

Gravel or ground cover of your choice

Plant notes: This plant is composed of 15 leaves, 10 large and 5 small, in a 10-inch-diameter [25.5-cm] pot. The approximate finished size is 15 inches high × 20 inches wide [38 × 51 cm].

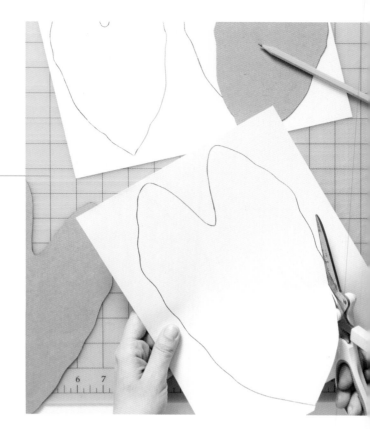

STEP 1

TRACE AND CUT OUT THE LEAVES.

Reserve 1 sheet of paper for making strips. Use the 2 templates to trace 10 large and 5 small leaf shapes on the remaining sheets of paper. Use scissors to cut out the leaves.

STEP 2

ADD DETAILS TO THE LEAVES.

Using the pattern on page 285 as a guide, use the dark green alcohol marker to draw details on each leaf. Then, soak a cotton swab in alcohol and trace it over every line so that the ink bleeds and further soaks into the paper.

STEP 3

CONNECT THE WIRES TO THE LEAVES AND COVER THE CONNECTION.

Cut the reserved sheet of paper into fifteen 1- × 4-inch [2.5- × 10-cm] strips. Place a large leaf pattern side down and position a 16-inch [41-cm] wire in the center of the leaf, overlapping the paper by about 4 inches [10 cm] with the remainder of the wire protruding from the center of the crevice of the leaf shape. Following the instructions on page 42 for the paper strip method, cover the wire with a paper strip. The strip should be positioned ½ to 1 inch [12 mm to 2.5 cm] from the center of the crevice. Secure the wire in place by pressing the bone folder around the contours of the wire. Repeat for all the large leaves. Next, using wire cutters, cut 5 lengths of wire at 10 to 12 inches [25.5 to 30.5 cm] long. Repeat these steps to connect the wires to the small leaves.

STEP 4

ADD DETAILS TO THE PAPER STRIP.

Once the glue has dried fully, repeat the instructions in step 2. Use the dark green alcohol marker to connect the lines that have bled through the back of the leaf to the paper strip. Complete the effect by tracing an alcohol-soaked cotton swab over the new lines.

In one hand, hold a leaf firmly where the wire is attached to the leaf. Bend the length of wire down with your other hand, arching the stem just above where it connects to the leaf. Repeat for all the leaves. Insert the wire stems into the vessel prepared with foam, placing each one at a slightly different angle. Cover the foam with ground cover.

Calathea orbifolia

This stunner, a large-growing variety from Bolivia, is a member of a group of plants commonly known as "prayer plants." Its large round leaves are lined with thin-to-thick pale green stripes that can be easily duplicated with a brush. I love to add subtle touches of color to my plants—in this one I used two shades of green paper that are close in color value in order to mimic the lighter shade of green often seen on younger calathea leaves. This is a bigger specimen—the instructions that follow will create a 2½-foot [76-cm] wide plant. Get ready for her to be the main attraction!

TOOLS

Pencil

Scissors

Bone folder

Palette

Small liner and ¼-inch [6-mm] flat paintbrushes

Container for glue

MATERIALS

Template (page 279)

15 sheets of 8½- × 11-inch [21.5- × 28-cm] medium green text-weight paper

4 sheets of 8½- × 11-inch [21.5- × 28-cm] ochre-green text-weight paper

White and green gouache paints

Seventeen 16-inch [41-cm] lengths of 16-gauge green straight floral wire

White glue

Vessel prepared with foam

Gravel or ground cover of your choice (optional)

Plant notes: This plant is composed of 17 leaves, 3 ochre-green and 14 medium green, in a 9- × 9-inch-wide [23-cm] basket. The approximate finished size is 24 inches high × 30 inches wide [61 × 76 cm].

STEP 1

TRACE AND CUT OUT THE LEAVES.

Reserve 1 sheet of paper in each color for making strips. Use the template to trace 14 medium green and 3 ochre-green leaf shapes on the remaining sheets of paper. Use scissors to cut out the leaves.

STEP 2

FOLD THE LEAVES IN HALF.

Fold each leaf in half lengthwise, making sure that the crease meets up with the point of the leaf at the base and the small crevice at the center of the leaf at the top. Use a bone folder to press each crease.

STEP 3

PAINT A CENTER VEIN.

Mix green and white gouache paint to create a pale green color and lightly dilute the paint with water. Using a liner paintbrush, paint a thin line down the center of each leaf, starting at the base (the pointy end). Painting a straight line is easier if you hold the paper in a slight fold in order to create a "ditch" to paint in.

STEP 4

ADD DETAILS TO THE LEAVES.

Using pale green gouache paint lightly diluted with water and a ¼-inch [6-mm] flat paintbrush, paint pairs of thin-to-thick wavy lines on each leaf. Varying the pressure on the paintbrush as you paint will help create the gradation in the thickness of the lines. (Practice the technique on a scrap piece of paper if you like.) Use the pattern for painting on page 284 as a guide, or paint each leaf freehand.

STEP 5

CONNECT THE WIRES TO THE LEAVES AND COVER THE CONNECTION.

Cut the reserved sheets of paper into seventeen 1- × 4-inch [2.5- × 10-cm] strips—one for each leaf (14 medium green and 3 ochre green). Place a large leaf pattern side down and position a 16-inch [41-cm] wire on the leaf, overlapping the paper by about 3 inches [7.5 cm] and following the center crease. The remainder of the wire should protrude from the point of the leaf shape. Following the instructions on page 42 for the paper strip method, cover the wire with a paper strip. The strip should be positioned flush with the leaf point. Secure the wire in place by pressing the bone folder around the contours of the wire. Once the glue is dry, trim the paper strip where it is visible from the front, following the contours of the leaf. Repeat for all the leaves.

STEP 6

SHAPE THE LEAVES AND STEMS.

Lightly curl the edges of some of the leaves to create visual interest and variety. Bend down the wires on most of the leaves, allowing the wire to bend just above where it connects to the paper, but leave the wires on 5 or 6 leaves straight.

Insert the wire stems into the vessel prepared with foam, placing the leaves with straight stems in the center, styling the others at slightly different angles, and mixing the ochre-colored leaves among the darker leaves. If the foam is visible, cover it with ground cover.

Pink Cordyline

The paper version I've made here is slightly smaller than the real plants that you'd find in a garden center. Its palm-like, or grassy, appearance is easy to duplicate with paper. I've used pale pink paper, but a hot or vibrant pink would also be true to life, as a variety of this plant is known as electric pink cordyline. This paper plant is a prime example of why you don't need real flowers to decorate your home—these pink blades would be fantastic in a long planter running down the center of a dining table.

TOOLS

Pencil

Ruler

X-Acto knife

Scissors

Wire cutters

Container for glue

¼-inch [6-mm] flat and small round paintbrushes

Bone folder

Palette

MATERIALS

Template (page 270)

2 sheets of 8½ × 11-inch [21.5- × 28-cm] pink cover-weight paper

1 sheet of 8½ × 11-inch [21.5- × 28-cm] pink text-weight paper

Nine 16-inch [41-cm] lengths of 20-gauge green straight floral wire

White glue

Black and green gouache paints

Vessel prepared with foam

Gravel or ground cover of your choice

Plant notes: This plant is composed of approximately 36 leaves in two sizes in a 4-inch-diameter [10-cm] pot. The approximate finished size is 10 inches high × 14 inches wide [25.5 × 35.5 cm].

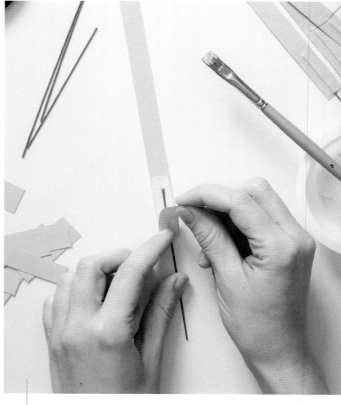

STEP 1

TRACE AND CUT OUT THE LEAVES.

Reserve the sheet of text-weight paper for making strips. With the cover-weight pieces of paper, use the template to trace the leaf shape on one piece of paper oriented vertically, and one piece of paper oriented horizontally with the template spanning the height of each page. Trace approximately 16 small and 20 large leaf shapes. Use a ruler and an X-Acto knife to cut the straight sides of the leaves and scissors to cut the pointy tips.

STEP 2

CONNECT THE WIRES TO THE LEAVES.

Cut the text-weight sheet of paper into thirty-six 1/2- × 2-inch [12-mm × 5-cm] strips. Use wire cutters to cut 36 lengths of wire at 3 to 4 inches [7.5 to 10 cm] long. Position a wire in the center of a leaf, overlapping the paper by about 1 1/2 inches [4 cm] with the remainder of the wire protruding from the base of the leaf shape. Following the instructions on page 42 for the paper strip method, cover the wire with a paper strip. The strip should be positioned flush with the base of the leaf. Secure the wire in place by pressing the bone folder around the contours of the wire. Repeat for all the leaves.

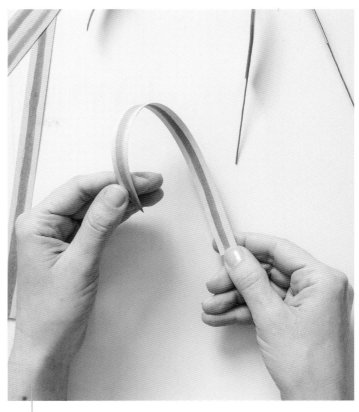

STEP 3

ADD DETAILS TO THE LEAVES.

Mix green and black gouache paint to create
a green-grey color and dilute the paint with
water. Test the color on a scrap piece of paper;
you want a pale, translucent consistency. Using
a small round paintbrush, paint a line down
the center of each leaf, starting from the base.
Once dry, paint a line down the center of the
other side.

STEP 4

SHAPE THE LEAVES.

Holding the base of a leaf (where the wire is
connected) firmly in one hand, pull the leaf
taut between the fingers of your other hand,
creating a slight curve to each leaf.

Starting in the center of the foam and
working out toward the outer edge, insert the
wire stems into the vessel prepared with foam,
placing each leaf at a slightly different angle.
Cover the foam with ground cover.

Angel Wing Begonia

"Angel wing" is the common name for several varieties of begonias. As a hobbyist plant grower, I often prefer the common name, even though it may be thought of as less accurate than the scientific name. Many common names are charming and descriptive, further endearing the plant to me. Like many begonias, this variety's leaves have a vibrant red underside, which is fun to execute in paper. The young leaves vary in color, starting off as a pale ochre-green with splotches of red and dark green. Each leaf has a splattering of bright white dots and wavy edges. Did you know that there is an American Begonia Society? It's true—some plants are so loved that people form societies dedicated to their study, development, and admiration. Or, they make them from paper!

TOOLS

Palette

1-inch [2.5-cm] flat and small round paintbrushes

Pencil

Wire cutters

Iron and ironing surface

Scissors

X-Acto knife

Large spray bottle filled with water

MATERIALS

3 templates (pages 272, 273)

Green and red acrylic paints

4 sheets of 8½- × 11-inch [21.5- × 28-cm] ochre-green text-weight paper

6 sheets of 8½- × 11-inch [21.5- × 28-cm] red text-weight paper

Twelve 16-inch [41-cm] lengths of 20-gauge green straight floral wire

2 sheets of 8½- × 11-inch [21.5- × 28-cm] dark green text-weight paper

6 sheets of iron-on adhesive cut to 8½ × 11 inches [21.5 × 28 cm]

White gouache paint

Two 16-inch [41-cm] lengths of 18-gauge green straight floral wire

Green floral tape

Vessel prepared with foam

Gravel or ground cover of your choice

Dowel; 22 inches [56 cm] long with a ¼-inch [6-mm] diameter (optional)

Plant notes: The draping specimen pictured on the previous page is composed of approximately 15 leaves of various sizes on a single vine, and the upright plant is made with about 24 leaves of various sizes on 3 stems of different lengths. Each is planted in 5- to 6-inch-high [13- to 15-cm] pot. The approximate finished size of each plant is 16 inches high × 12 inches wide [46 × 30.5 cm].

STEP 1

PREPARE THE PAPER.

Following the instructions on page 36 for making a wash, paint a wash of splotchy red and green acrylic paint on one side of each sheet of ochre-green paper. Allow the paper to dry fully. Leave the dark green and red paper unpainted.

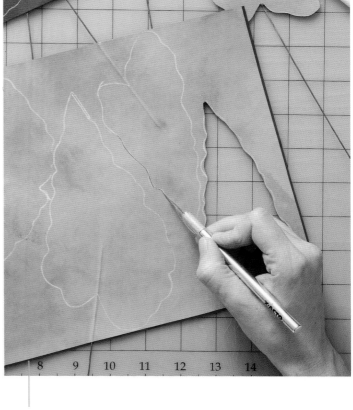

STEP 2

CONNECT THE WIRE AND PAPER.

Depending on which plant you are making, make 15 to 24 leaves of various sizes. Mock up the template placement on the red sheets of paper (fitting 4 to 5 leaves per sheet) and mark with a pencil where the wires will be placed. Using wire cutters, cut the 20-gauge wire into approximately 8-inch [20.5-cm] lengths, cutting enough wire to make 1 stem for each leaf. Make approximately 2 paper-and-wire sandwiches using red and dark green paper and 4 paper-and-wire sandwiches using red and painted-ochre paper (painted side facing out) by following the instructions on page 42 for the iron-on adhesive method.

STEP 3

TRACE AND CUT OUT THE LEAVES.

Position the 3 templates over the wires in the paper-and-wire sandwiches, making sure the wires protrude from the crevice in the base (not the pointy end) of the leaf shapes. Trace 15 to 24 leaf shapes in various sizes and colors and use scissors (or an X-Acto knife) to cut them out. If necessary, use an X-Acto knife to carefully cut the base of the leaf around the wire connection to release the paper that is adhered to the stem.

STEP 4

SHAPE THE LEAVES.

Following the instructions on page 51 for working with wet paper, shape each leaf by lightly misting both sides and forming the edges into uneven waves, pinching a portion at a time with your fingers. Form each leaf a little differently, and set them aside to dry fully.

STEP 5

ADD DETAILS TO THE LEAVES.

Using white gouache paint lightly diluted with water and a small round paintbrush, paint small dots on each leaf. Differ the pattern from leaf to leaf by painting fewer or more dots in various sizes.

STEP 6

CONNECT THE STEMS TO MAKE VINES AND SPRIGS.

Create a main stem with an 18-gauge 16-inch [41-cm] wire. Using green floral tape, wrap the stems of 2 smaller leaves to the end of the wire 1 to 2 inches [2.5 to 5 cm] from the base of each leaf. Continue to attach leaf stems at approximately 2-inch [5-cm] intervals as you work down the length of the wire. Alternate randomly between attaching large, medium, and small leaves until you have attached approximately 12 leaves. If making a larger plant, use wire cutters to cut two 6-inch [15-cm] lengths from the remaining piece of 18-gauge wire and use green floral tape to wrap 3 to 5 leaves to each to make 2 sprigs.

STEP 7

STYLE THE VINES AND SPRIGS.

Bend each leaf to alternating sides of the vine, occasionally pulling a leaf toward you and bending it to point down. Shape each vine and sprig slightly differently.

Assemble the plant by inserting the wire into the vessel prepared with foam. Shape your plant by gently bending the wires to drape down the side of the pot, or keep the plant upright. As a styling choice, I added a dowel to my upright plant. Cover the foam with ground cover.

Swiss Cheese Vine

Swiss cheese vine, also known as *Monstera obliqua*, is one of the plants I have long coveted and delighted in. I love how expressive and different each leaf is. The "Swiss cheese" holes always vary in size and location on the leaves, giving each leaf its own personality. It takes patience and finger strength to cut out all the holes, but the results are worth it. I've styled the plant in a pot, but it would also look great in a hanging basket, or in any place where it can show off its flamboyant character.

TOOLS

Pencil

Wire cutters

Iron and ironing surface

Scissors

X-Acto knife

Large spray bottle
with water

Hot-glue gun and
glue sticks

MATERIALS

5 templates (page 271)

19 sheets of 8½- × 11-inch
[21.5- × 28-cm] medium
green text-weight paper

Eighteen 16-inch [41-cm]
lengths of 20-gauge green
straight floral wire

9 sheets of iron-on adhesive
cut to 8½ × 11 inches
[21.5 × 28 cm]

Kraft paper

Green floral tape

Four 16-inch [41-cm] lengths
of 18-gauge green straight
floral wire

Vessel prepared with foam

Gravel or ground cover of
your choice (optional)

Plant notes: This plant is composed of approximately 36 leaves in two sizes. It consists of 3 vines of various lengths with 5 to 12 leaves each, 6 sprigs with 3 to 4 leaves each, and 3 to 5 baby leaves, all in a 6-inch-diameter [15-cm] pot. The approximate finished size is 20 inches high × 15 inches wide [51 × 38 cm].

STEP 1

CONNECT THE WIRE AND PAPER.

Reserve 1 sheet of paper to make baby leaves. Using the remaining sheets of paper, mock up the template placement for approximately 18 each of the large and small leaves (fitting about 4 leaves per sheet) and mark with a pencil where the wires will be placed. Using wire cutters, cut the 20-gauge wire into 36 lengths approximately 8 inches [20.5 cm] long. Make paper-and-wire sandwiches by following the instructions on page 42 for the iron-on adhesive method.

STEP 2

TRACE AND CUT OUT THE LEAVES.

Position the 2 leaf templates over the wires in the paper-and-wire sandwiches, making sure the wires protrude from the crevice in the base (not the pointy end) of the leaf shapes. Trace approximately 18 each of the large and small leaf shapes and use scissors (or an X-Acto knife) to cut them out. If necessary, use an X-Acto knife to carefully cut around the wire at the base of the leaf to release the paper that is adhered to the stem. Use the 3 oval templates to trace several holes in each leaf, varying the sizes and positions from leaf to leaf (or draw freehand). Use an X-Acto knife to cut out the ovals.

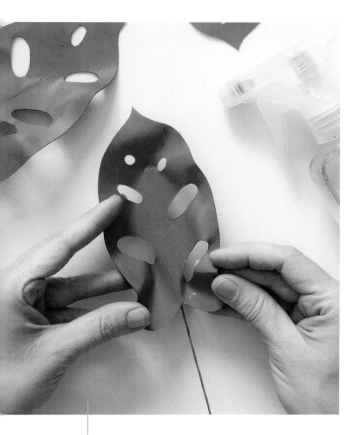

STEP 3

SHAPE THE LEAF.

Following the instructions on page 51 for work-ing with wet paper, shape each leaf by lightly misting both sides and forming the edges into uneven waves, pinching a portion at a time with your fingers. Form each leaf a little differ-ently, and set them aside to dry fully.

STEP 4

CRAFT BABY LEAVES.

Following the instructions on page 59 for mak-ing baby leaves, craft 3 to 5 baby leaves out of the reserved sheet of paper. For each leaf, tear off a small triangular piece of brown kraft paper and use the hot-glue gun to attach it over the connection you made with floral tape.

CONNECT THE STEMS TO MAKE SPRIGS.

Using wire cutters, cut four 5-inch [13-cm] lengths from the 18-gauge wire. Using green floral tape, wrap the stems of 2 leaves to the end of 1 of the wires 1 to 2 inches [2.5 to 5 cm] from the base of each leaf. Continue to attach leaf stems at approximately 1-inch [2.5-cm] intervals as you work down the length of the wire, until you've attached 3 or 4 leaves. Wrap a small piece of kraft paper around a few of the connections using a hot-glue gun. Repeat to make 4 sprigs.

CONNECT THE STEMS TO MAKE VINES.

Create a vine with an 18-gauge 16-inch [41-cm] wire. Using green floral tape, wrap the stems of 2 leaves to the end of the wire 1 to 2 inches [2.5 to 5 cm] from the base of each leaf. Continue to attach leaf stems at approximately 1-inch [2.5-cm] intervals as you work down the length of the wire. Alternate randomly between attaching large and small leaves until you have attached approximately 12 leaves. Using wire cutters, cut two 6-inch [15-cm] lengths of 18-gauge wire and repeat these steps to attach approximately 5 leaves to each to make 2 more vines. Wrap a small piece of kraft paper around a few of the connections using a hot-glue gun.

Assemble the plant by inserting the wires into the vessel prepared with foam. Shape the plant so that the longer vine drapes down the side of the pot, then fill in with the shorter vines and sprigs. If the foam is visible, cover it with ground cover.

Rattlesnake Plant

This superstar's common name hints at its lance-shaped leaf's showy ornamentation, a quality for which it is desired. Dark green painterly dots adorn a light green background with vibrant red or burgundy undersides. This plant moves and lifts its leaves in the evening to reveal its red coloring. The movement is called nyctinastic movement, and scientists suspect that it happens for the protection of the plant, although this is still being studied. But, if you'd like your paper version to be nyctinastic and fantastic, you'll need to bend the wires yourself!

TOOLS

Pencil

Wire cutters

Iron and ironing surface

Scissors

Palette

Small round and liner paintbrushes

Large spray bottle with water

MATERIALS

3 templates (page 277)

5 sheets of 8½- × 11-inch [21.5- × 28-cm] red text-weight paper

Ten 16-inch [41-cm] lengths of 20-gauge red straight floral wire

5 sheets of 8½- × 11-inch [21.5- × 28-cm] chartreuse text-weight paper

5 sheets of iron-on adhesive cut to 8½ × 11 inches [21.5 × 28 cm]

Dark green acrylic paint

Vessel prepared with foam

Gravel or ground cover of your choice

Plant notes: This plant is composed of approximately 20 leaves in three sizes in a 4-inch-diameter [10-cm] pot. The approximate finished size is 14 inches high × 10 inches wide [35.5 × 25.5 cm].

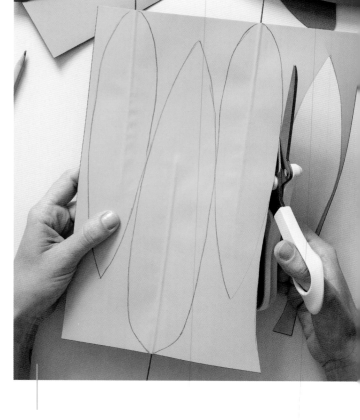

STEP 1

CONNECT THE WIRE AND PAPER.

Mock up the template placement for approximately 10 large, 7 medium, and 3 small leaves on the red sheets of paper (fitting about 4 leaves per sheet) and mark with a pencil where the wires will be placed. Using wire cutters, cut the 20-gauge wire into 20 lengths approximately 8 inches [20.5 cm] long. Make paper-and-wire sandwiches using red and chartreuse paper by following the instructions on page 42 for the iron-on adhesive method.

STEP 2

TRACE AND CUT OUT THE LEAVES.

Position the 3 templates over the wires in the paper-and-wire sandwiches, making sure the wires protrude from the center of the base (not the pointy end) of the leaf shapes. Trace approximately 10 large, 7 medium, and 3 small leaf shapes and use scissors to cut them out.

STEP 3

ADD DETAILS TO THE LEAVES.

Dilute dark green acrylic paint with water. Test the color on a scrap piece of paper; you want a pale, translucent consistency. Using the liner paintbrush, paint two parallel lines down the center of each leaf by running the brush along the edge of either side of the wire. Next, use a small round paintbrush to paint teardrop shapes in various sizes on both halves of the leaf. Use the pattern for painting on page 287 as a guide, or paint each leaf freehand.

STEP 4

SHAPE THE LEAVES.

Following the instructions on page 51 for working with wet paper, shape each leaf by lightly misting both sides and forming the edges into uneven waves, pinching a portion at a time with your fingers. Add gentle waves to the wire inside the leaf as well. Form each leaf slightly differently, and set them aside to dry.

Insert the wires into the vessel prepared with foam, starting in the center and working out toward the outer edge. Arrange the leaves at varying angles so that a few of the leaves show their red undersides. Cover the foam with ground cover.

Arrowhead Vine

I made this plant based on a six-year-old houseplant a friend of mine has. She claims that she just waters it and walks away, and yet it looks pretty much like this paper version—happy and lush. Some people are just lucky! The leaves are a subtle shade of blue-green, and they are deeply folded to create a three-dimensional shape. This shape allows for nuanced brightness and shadow, depending on how light hits the leaves. When making a vine plant, I often will make one side longer than the other. I think it helps keep my pot from looking like it is wearing a plant wig!

TOOLS

Scissors

X-Acto knife

Wire cutters

Pencil

1-inch [2.5-cm] flat
paintbrush

Palette

Iron and ironing surface

Large spray bottle
with water

MATERIALS

3 templates (page 259)

Blue acrylic paint

14 sheets of 8½- × 11-inch
[21.5- × 28-cm] medium
green text-weight paper

7 sheets of iron-on adhesive
cut to 8½ × 11 inches
[21.5 × 28 cm]

Twelve 16-inch [41-cm] lengths
of 20-gauge green straight
floral wire

Five 16-inch [41-cm] lengths
of 18-gauge green straight
floral wire

Green floral tape

Vessel prepared with foam

Gravel or ground cover
of your choice

Plant notes: This plant is composed of approximately 35 leaves in three sizes. It consists of 3 vines of various lengths with 5 to 8 leaves each, and 5 sprigs with 2 to 4 leaves each, all in a 6-inch-diameter [15-cm] pot. The approximate finished size is 20 inches high × 16 inches wide [51 × 41 cm].

STEP 1

PREPARE THE PAPER.

Following the instructions on page 36 for making a wash, paint a wash of blue acrylic paint on one side of each sheet of medium green paper. Allow the paper to dry fully.

STEP 2

CONNECT THE WIRE AND PAPER.

Mock up the template placement for approximately 20 large, 10 medium, and 5 small leaves on the unpainted side of the paper (fitting about 5 leaves per sheet) and mark with a pencil where the wires will be placed. Use wire cutters to cut the 20-gauge wire into 35 lengths, approximately 5 inches [13 cm] long. Make paper-and-wire sandwiches using the painted paper (painted side facing out) by following the instructions on page 42 for the iron-on adhesive method.

STEP 3

TRACE AND CUT OUT THE LEAVES.

Position the 3 templates over the wires in the paper-and-wire sandwiches, making sure the wires protrude from the crevice in the base (not the pointy end) of the leaf shapes. Trace approximately 20 large, 10 medium, and 5 small leaf shapes and use scissors (or an X-Acto knife) to cut them out. If necessary, use an X-Acto knife to carefully cut around the wire at the base of the leaf to release the paper that is adhered to the stem.

STEP 4

SHAPE THE LEAVES.

Following the instructions on page 51 for working with wet paper, shape each leaf with water. First, lightly mist both sides of a leaf, then pinch the bottom and each point with your fingers to give the leaf a deep Y-shaped crevice. Repeat for all the leaves and set aside to dry fully.

STEP 5

CONNECT THE STEMS TO MAKE SPRIGS.

Using wire cutters, cut five 5-inch [13-cm] lengths of 18-gauge wire. Using green floral tape, wrap the stems of 2 leaves to a wire 1 to 2 inches [2.5 to 5 cm] from the base of each leaf. Continue to attach leaf stems at approximately 1-inch [2.5-cm] intervals as you work down the length of the wire until you have attached 2 to 4 leaves per wire. Repeat to make 5 sprigs.

STEP 6

CONNECT THE STEMS TO MAKE VINES.

Create a vine with an 18-gauge 16-inch [41-cm] wire. Using green floral tape, wrap the stem of 1 leaf to the end of a wire 1 to 2 inches [2.5 to 5 cm] from the base of the leaf. Continue to attach leaf stems to the wire, one at a time, at approximately 2-inch [5-cm] intervals as you work down the length of the wire. Alternate randomly between attaching large, medium, and small leaves until you have attached 5 to 8 leaves. Using wire cutters, cut two 10-inch [25.5-cm] lengths of 18-gauge wire and repeat these steps to attach approximately 5 leaves to each to make 2 more vines.

Assemble the plant by inserting the longest vine at one side of the vessel prepared with foam with a medium-length vine next to it. Position the other medium vine on the opposite side of the pot and fill in with the sprigs. Cover the foam with ground cover.

Fishbone Cactus

Fishbone cacti grow in southern Mexico, in the nooks and crannies of trees in the humid rainforest. Similar to orchids, they root in the decaying matter that accumulates in the crevices of branches. To make this specimen, we'll use 8½- × 11-inch [21.5- × 28-cm] paper, but if you want the stems to trail even longer, you can use oversize paper. These guys can get quite long! I once saw a fishbone stem growing down the entire trunk of a tree in Oaxaca, making the tree look like it had a zipper!

TOOLS

Pencil

Bone folder

X-Acto knife

MATERIALS

Template (page 269)

10 sheets of 8½- × 11-inch [21.5- × 28-cm] medium green text-weight paper

5 sheets of double-sided adhesive cut to 8½ × 11 inches [21.5 × 28 cm]

Fifteen 16-inch [41-cm] lengths of 20-gauge green straight floral wire

Vessel prepared with foam

Gravel or ground cover of your choice

Plant notes: This plant is composed of 15 leaves in a 5-inch-diameter [13-cm] pot. The approximate finished size is 14 inches high × 14 inches wide [35.5 × 35.5 cm].

STEP 1

CONNECT THE WIRE AND PAPER.

Mock up the template placement for 15 leaves
(fitting 3 leaves per sheet) and mark with a
pencil where the 16-inch [41-cm] wires will be
placed, positioning the wires to span nearly the
entire length of each leaf. Make paper-and-wire
sandwiches by following the instructions on
page 45 for the double-sided adhesive method.

STEP 2

SECURE THE WIRE.

After you have made the paper-and-wire
sandwich, secure the wire in place by pressing
around the contours of the wire with a bone
folder—press around each side of the wire on
both sides of the paper.

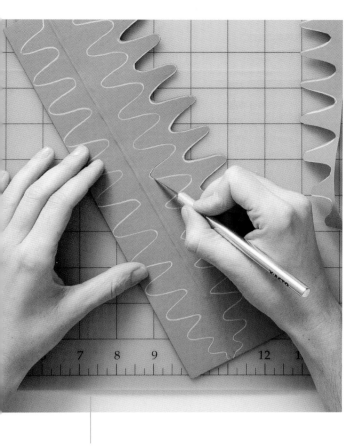

STEP 3

TRACE AND CUT OUT THE LEAVES.

Position the template over the wires in the paper-and-wire sandwiches, making sure the wires protrude from the center of the base (not the pointy end) of the leaf shapes. Trace 15 leaf shapes and use an X-Acto knife to cut them out.

STEP 4

SHAPE THE LEAVES.

Grasping a leaf in both hands, bend the wire to make a gentle curve in the leaf. Shape each leaf slightly differently.

Assemble the plant by placing the wire stems into the vessel prepared with foam, varying the angle of the leaves. Cover the foam with ground cover.

Pink Polka Dot Plant

You can make pale pink leaves like I have here, or go bold with hot pink or red leaves. A paper version of this plant is ideal, because a live pink polka dot plant typically needs bright sun to retain its spots—indoors, low light can cause its leaves to revert to solid green. This paper plant would be very cute in votive-size pots. The small delicate leaves are ornate enough to stand on their own as just a stem or two.

TOOLS

Pencil

Wire cutters

Bone folder

Scissors

MATERIALS

2 templates (page 258)

14 sheets of 8½- × 11-inch [21.5- × 28-cm] pink text-weight paper

1 sheet of 8½- × 11-inch [21.5- × 28-cm] hot pink text-weight paper

8 sheets of double-sided adhesive cut to 8½ × 11 inches [21.5 × 28 cm]

24-gauge spool wire

Hot pink and dark green alcohol markers

White gel pen

Ten 16-inch [41-cm] lengths of 20-gauge brown straight floral wire

Brown floral tape

Vessel prepared with foam

Gravel or ground cover of your choice

Plant notes: This plant is composed of approximately 200 leaves in two sizes in pink and hot pink on 20 stems in a 4-inch-diameter [10-cm] pot. The approximate finished size is 7 inches high × 12 inches wide [18 × 30.5 cm].

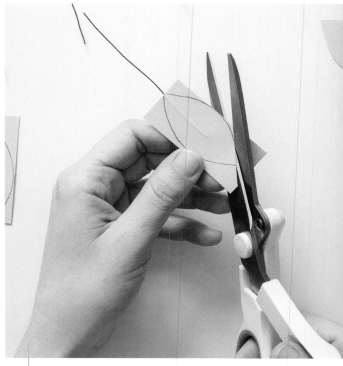

STEP 1

CONNECT THE WIRE AND PAPER TO MAKE LEAVES.

Because you are making small leaves, cut the paper and double-sided sheets in half twice so you have strips measuring 8$\frac{1}{2}$ × 2$\frac{3}{4}$ inches [21.5 × 7 cm]. Mock up the template placement for approximately 100 each of the large and small leaves (fitting 6 to 9 leaves per strip) and mark with a pencil where the wires will be placed. Using wire cutters, cut the 24-gauge spool wire into 200 lengths approximately 3 inches [7.5 cm] long. Make paper-and-wire sandwiches by following the instructions on page 45 for the double-sided adhesive method. Secure the wires in place by pressing the bone folder around the contours of each wire.

STEP 2

TRACE AND CUT OUT THE LEAVES.

Position the 2 templates over the wires in the paper-and-wire sandwiches, making sure the wires protrude from one point of the leaf shapes. Trace approximately 100 each of the large and small leaf shapes and use scissors to cut them out.

CONNECT THE STEMS TO MAKE SPRIGS.

Using wire cutters, cut twenty 8-inch [20.5-cm] lengths of 20-gauge wire. Position 1 leaf stem flush with the end of an 8-inch wire and, using brown floral tape, wrap the leaf stem to the wire. Continue to attach leaf stems to the wire, one at a time, at approximately 1/2-inch [12-mm] intervals as you work down the length of the wire. Alternate randomly between attaching large and small leaves until you have attached 6 to 12 leaves. Repeat to make 20 sprigs.

Assemble your plant by inserting the stems into the vessel prepared with foam. You can give some of the sprigs a slight curve if you like. Adjust the angle of the leaves so that the patterned side is facing out. If the foam is visible, cover it with ground cover.

ADD DETAILS TO THE LEAVES.

Using the hot pink and dark green alcohol markers, add irregular dots and splotches to one side of each leaf. Next, draw a line down the center of the leaf with a white gel pen. Repeat for all the leaves.

Swallowtail Plant

Christia obcordata, or swallowtail plant, is an obscure tropical plant with striped, triangular-shaped, fluttering leaves on thin stems. Highly coveted by plant enthusiasts, the swallowtail is hard to come by unless you live in Asia. In recent years, though, it's been showing up in select nurseries and is gaining in popularity worldwide. A paper version was a must, and I am pleased with how it turned out. The inherent delicateness of the wire mimics the thin stems of this plant and allows the leaves to quiver in the breeze.

TOOLS

Scissors

Pencil

Wire cutters

Bone folder

MATERIALS

3 templates (page 270)

8 sheets of 8½- × 11-inch [21.5- × 28-cm] medium green text-weight paper

4 sheets of double-sided adhesive cut to 8½ × 11 inches [21.5 × 28 cm]

Eighteen 16-inch [41-cm] lengths of 20-gauge green straight floral wire

Red alcohol marker

White gel pen

Green floral tape

Vessel prepared with foam

Gravel or ground cover of your choice

Plant notes: This plant is composed of approximately 42 leaves of various sizes on 6 stems, all in a 3-inch-diameter [7.5-cm] pot. The approximate finished size is 11 inches high × 13 inches wide [28 × 33 cm].

STEP 1

CONNECT THE WIRE AND PAPER.

Because you are making small leaves, cut the paper and double-sided adhesive sheets in half so that you have strips measuring 4¹/₄ × 11 inches [11 × 28 cm]. Mock up the template placement for approximately 20 large, 12 medium, and 5 small leaves (fitting about 6 leaves per strip) and mark with a pencil where the wires will be placed. Using wire cutters, cut 14 of the wires into 42 lengths approximately 5 inches [13 cm] long. Make paper-and-wire sandwiches by following the instructions on page 45 for the double-sided adhesive method. Secure the wires in place by pressing the bone folder around the contours of each wire.

STEP 2

TRACE AND CUT OUT THE LEAVES.

Position the 3 templates over the wires in the paper-and-wire sandwiches, making sure the wires protrude from center of the pointy base of the leaf shapes. Trace approximately 20 large, 12 medium, and 10 small leaf shapes and use scissors to cut them out.

STEP 3

ADD DETAILS TO THE LEAVES.

Using the red alcohol marker, and the pattern on page 287 as a guide, draw one dotted line down the center of a leaf (along the concealed wire) and several dotted lines branching off from each side. Next, using a white gel pen, draw a line down the center of each of the dotted lines. Repeat on the front and back of all the leaves.

STEP 4

CONNECT THE STEMS TO MAKE SPRIGS.

Using wire cutters, cut three 10-inch [25.5-cm] lengths of 20-gauge wire. Using green floral tape, wrap the stem of 1 leaf to the end of a wire 1 to 2 inches [2.5 to 5 cm] from the base of the leaf. Continue to attach leaf stems to the wire, one at a time, at 1- to 2-inch [2.5- to 5-cm] intervals as you work down the length of the wire. Alternate randomly between attaching large, medium, and small leaves until you have attached 7 to 8 leaves. Repeat to make 3 sprigs. Use the leftover 6-inch [15-cm] lengths of 20-gauge wire to repeat these steps to make 3 more sprigs with 4 to 6 leaves each.

If you like, give some of the sprigs a gentle curve by bending the straight floral wire slightly. Assemble the plant by inserting the stems into the vessel prepared with foam. Cover the foam with ground cover.

Variegated Lady Palm

Another on my list of rare plants deserving of a paper version, the variegated lady palm, or dwarf *Rhapis excelsa,* has been cultivated in Japan and is so prized that it is often passed down through generations. Elsewhere, the collecting of these plants is relegated to plant fanatics! Variegated varieties exist in assorted shades: green and cream, green and yellow, or light and dark green. When researching this plant, I was most enamored with the light and dark green. It's so chic!

TOOLS

1-inch [2.5-cm] chip brush

Palette

Pencil

Bone folder

Scissors

MATERIALS

Template (page 267)

12 sheets of 8½- × 11-inch [21.5- × 28-cm] pale green text-weight paper

Green acrylic paint

Thirty 16-inch [41-cm] lengths of 20-gauge dark green straight floral wire

6 sheets of double-sided adhesive cut to 8½ × 11 inches [21.5 × 28 cm]

Dark green floral tape

Three 16-inch [41-cm] lengths of 16-gauge dark green straight floral wire

Vessel prepared with foam

Gravel or ground cover of your choice

Plant notes: This plant is composed of 30 leaves to make 10 palms in a 9-inch-diameter [23-cm] pot. The approximate finished size is 22 inches high × 19 inches wide [56 × 48 cm].

STEP 1

PREPARE THE PAPER.

Orient a sheet of pale green paper vertically and, following the instructions on page 36 for the dry-brush technique, paint horizontal stripes across one side of the paper using a 1-inch [2.5-cm] chip brush and green acrylic paint. Repeat for each sheet of pale green paper. Allow the paper to dry fully.

STEP 2

CONNECT THE WIRE AND PAPER.

Mock up the template placement for 30 leaves on the unpainted side of the paper (fitting 5 leaves per sheet) and mark with a pencil where the 16-inch [41-cm] 20-gauge wires will be placed, making sure the wires are parallel to the painted stripes. Make paper-and-wire sandwiches with the painted sides facing out by following the instructions on page 45 for the double-sided adhesive method. Secure the wires in place by pressing the bone folder around the contours of each wire.

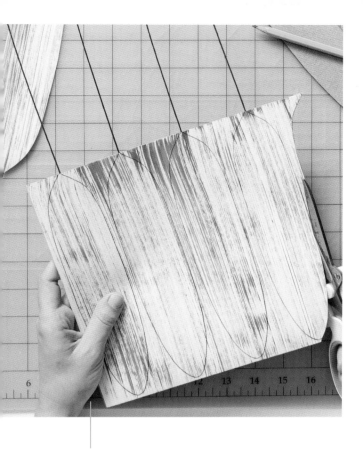

STEP 3

TRACE AND CUT OUT THE LEAVES.

Position the template over the wires in the paper-and-wire sandwiches, making sure the wires protrude from the center of the pointy base of the leaf shapes. Trace 30 leaf shapes and use scissors to cut them out.

STEP 4

CONNECT THE STEMS TO MAKE A PALM.

Stack 3 leaves on top of each other. Using dark green floral tape, tape the 3 stems together, covering the stems entirely. You now have a palm. Repeat with the remaining leaves to make 10 palms.

STEP 5

CREATE PALM BRANCHES.

Set 1 palm aside to be inserted into the pot as a stand-alone palm. Make a palm branch by attaching 3 palms to 1 of the 16-gauge wires, staggering their positions so that 2 of the palms extend above the 16-gauge wire and 1 palm is attached approximately 4 inches [10 cm] below the end of the 16-gauge wire, and wrapping them together with green floral tape. Repeat for with the remaining palms to make 3 palm branches. Fully cover the stems and wire with floral tape.

STEP 6

SHAPE THE PALMS.

Spread the 3 leaves of each palm apart at an equal distance, and bend 1 palm so that it points down. Spread the palm branches to either side as well.

Insert the 3 branches and 1 reserved palm into the vessel prepared with foam. Cover the foam with ground cover.

Never-Never Plant

For the longest time, I thought this plant was a philodendron pink princess. They share the same gorgeous green and pink colors and are a similar size. Finally, a plant buddy of mine set me straight. It is a never-never plant, or *Ctenanthe oppenheimiana* tricolor. I am partial to "never-never," however. I like to think it's named that because it is young at heart, like me and Peter Pan! This is a good plant on which to practice your gouache-paint application skills; each leaf is slightly different, so there are no mistakes.

TOOLS

Pencil

Bone folder

Scissors

Palette

½-inch [12-mm] flat paintbrush

Hot-glue gun and glue sticks

Wire cutters

MATERIALS

3 templates (page 254)

3 sheets of 8½- × 11-inch [21.5- × 28-cm] hot pink text-weight paper

10 sheets of 8½- × 11-inch [21.5- × 28-cm] pale pink text-weight paper

2 sheets of 8½- × 11-inch [21.5- × 28-cm] dark green text-weight paper

7 sheets of double-sided adhesive cut to 8½ × 11 inches [21.5 × 28 cm]

Forty 16-inch [41-cm] lengths of 20-gauge green straight floral wire

Green, red, and white gouache paints

Pink floral tape

Vessel prepared with foam

Gravel or ground cover of your choice

Plant notes: This plant is composed of approximately 35 leaves of various sizes in pink, hot pink, and dark green, as well as 3 to 5 baby leaves, all in a 5-inch-diameter [13-cm] pot. The approximate finished size is 16 inches high × 19 inches wide [41 × 48 cm].

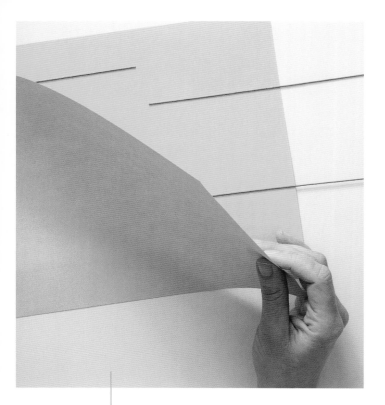

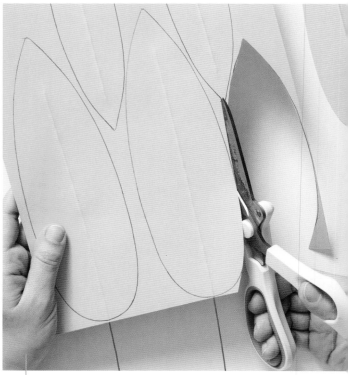

STEP 1

CONNECT THE WIRE AND PAPER.

Reserve 1 sheet of hot pink paper to make baby leaves. Using the remaining sheets of paper, mock up the template placement for approximately 20 large, 10 medium, and 5 small leaves (fitting about 5 leaves per sheet) and mark with a pencil where the 16-inch [41-cm] wires will be placed. Make 5 pale pink, 1 hot pink, and 1 dark green paper-and-wire sandwiches by following the instructions on page 45 for the double-sided adhesive method. Secure the wires in place by pressing the bone folder around the contours of each wire.

STEP 2

TRACE AND CUT OUT THE LEAVES.

Position the 3 templates over the wires in the paper-and-wire sandwiches, making sure the wires protrude from the center of the base (not the pointy end) of the leaf shapes. Trace approximately 20 large, 10 medium, and 5 small leaf shapes and use scissors to cut them out.

STEP 3

ADD DETAILS TO THE LEAVES.

Mix green and white gouache paint to create pale green and medium green colors and lightly dilute the paint with water. Using a ½-inch [12-mm] flat paintbrush, paint wide arching strokes away from the centerline of each pink and hot pink leaf. Mix red and white gouache paint to create a bright pink color, lightly dilute the paint with water, and paint wide arching strokes away from the centerline of each green leaf. Differ the pattern from leaf to leaf by painting fewer or more strokes in various sizes and shades.

STEP 4

CRAFT BABY LEAVES AND TAPE THE STEMS.

Following the instructions on page 59 for making baby leaves, make 3 to 5 baby leaves on 8-inch [20.5-cm] stems in different sizes using the remaining sheet of hot pink paper. Wrap pink floral tape around the stems of the baby leaves, then wrap the stems of all the leaves with pink floral tape.

Assemble the plant by inserting a few stems into the vessel prepared with foam leaving the stems straight. Bend the other stems down at various angles and insert them in the foam, arranging the leaves at various angles. Cover the foam with ground cover.

Inch Plant

The inch plant has the scientific name of *Tradescantia zebrina*. I remember it from my childhood, as a ground cover my parents planted under the oak tree in our yard. Lately, I have seen it as a trailing plant in pots indoors and out. The leaves along the stem are generally 1 inch apart, hence the common name. The inch plant can grow vines up to 6 feet [1.8 m] long. If you'd like to get that impressive with your paper version, make sure you have plenty of floral tape on hand!

TOOLS

Palette

Large spray bottle with water

¼-inch [6-mm] flat, 1-inch [2.5-cm] flat paintbrushes

Scissors

Pencil

Wire cutters

Bone folder

MATERIALS

2 templates (page 255)

Black acrylic paint

9 sheets of 8½- × 11-inch [21.5- × 28-cm] dark green text-weight paper

9 sheets of 8½- × 11-inch [21.5- × 28-cm] maroon text-weight paper

9 sheets of double-sided adhesive cut to 8½ × 11 inches [21.5 × 28 cm]

Sixty-four 16-inch [41-cm] lengths of 20-gauge green straight floral wire

Red and white gouache paints

Dark green floral tape

Vessel prepared with foam

Gravel or ground cover of your choice

Plant notes: This plant is composed of approximately 132 leaves in two sizes. It consists of 5 vines of various lengths with 8 to 20 leaves each, and 12 sprigs with 4 to 6 leaves each, all in a 4-inch-diameter [10-cm] pot. The approximate finished size is 20 inches high × 13 inches wide [51 × 33 cm].

STEP 1

PREPARE THE PAPER.

Following the instructions on page 36 for making a wash, paint a wash of black acrylic paint on 1 side of each sheet of dark green paper. Allow the paper to dry fully. Leave the maroon paper unpainted.

STEP 2

CONNECT THE WIRE AND PAPER.

Because you are making small leaves, cut the paper and double-sided sheets in half so you have strips measuring 4¼ × 11 inches [11 × 28 cm]. Mock up the template placement for approximately 68 each of the large and small leaves on the maroon paper (fitting 8 to 10 leaves per strip) and mark with a pencil where the wires will be placed. Using wire cutters, cut 44 of the 20-gauge wires into 132 lengths approximately 5 inches [13 cm] long. Make paper-and-wire sandwiches using the maroon and painted paper (painted side facing out) by following the instructions on page 45 for the double-sided adhesive method. Secure the wires in place by pressing the bone folder around the contours of each wire.

STEP 3

TRACE AND CUT OUT THE LEAVES.

Position the 2 templates over the wires in the paper-and-wire sandwiches, making sure the wires protrude from the center of the base (not the pointy end) of the leaf shapes. Trace approximately 68 each of the large and small leaves and use scissors to cut them out.

STEP 4

ADD DETAILS TO THE LEAVES.

Mix red and white gouache paint to create a pale pink color and lightly dilute the paint with water. On the green side of each leaf, use a 1/4-inch [6-mm] flat paintbrush to paint several arching strokes from the base to the tip following the contour of the leaf and tapering the strokes toward the tip.

STEP 5

CONNECT THE STEMS TO MAKE VINES AND SPRIGS.

Create a 22-inch [56-cm] vine by overlapping and taping two 20-gauge wires together with dark green floral tape. Then, position the base of 1 leaf flush with the end of the 22-inch wire and wrap it to the wire with the dark green floral tape. Continue to attach leaf stems to the wire, one at a time, at approximately 1-inch [2.5-cm] intervals, alternating sides as you work down the length of the wire. Alternate randomly between attaching large and small leaves until you have attached approximately 20 leaves. Repeat these steps to create two 22-inch [56-cm] long vines. Using wire cutters, cut three 10-inch [25.5-cm] lengths of 20-gauge wire and repeat these steps to create three 10-inch vines with approximately 8 leaves each. Then, cut twelve 6-inch [15-cm] lengths of 20-gauge wire and, still using dark green floral tape, wrap 4 to 6 leaves to each length to create 12 sprigs.

STEP 6

STYLE THE VINES AND SPRIGS.

Bend the leaves down until they're almost perpendicular to the vine wire. Shape the vines into a subtle zigzag by bending the vine wire gently at the point where each leaf stem is connected.

Assemble the plant by inserting the vines into the foam on one side of the vessel and filling in the rest of the vessel with the shorter sprigs. Cover the foam with ground cover.

Philodendron billietiae

Extremely rare, *Philodendron billietiae* is found only in French Guiana and northern Brazil and wasn't discovered until 2006. When I learned about this plant, I was so struck by its vibrant orange stems and elongated leaves that I had to make it out of paper. The young plants have smaller leaves, and those are what I've made here. However, a mature plant can grow leaves upwards of 3 feet [1 m] long. I'll feel lucky if I ever get to see one of these in person!

TOOLS

Pencil

Bone folder

Scissors

X-Acto knife

Utility knife

Wire cutters

Clippers

Small round paintbrush

Containers for glue and paint

Hot-glue gun and glue sticks

MATERIALS

2 templates (page 263)

1 sheet of 8½- × 11-inch [21.5- × 28-cm] ochre-green text-weight paper

Ten 16-inch [41-cm] lengths of 18-gauge straight floral wire

Orange floral tape

11 sheets of 8½- × 11-inch [21.5- × 28-cm] dark green text-weight paper

5 sheets of double-sided adhesive cut to 8½ × 11 inches [21.5 × 28 cm]

Hot pink and lime green gel pens

Skewers

Foam

Kraft paper

White glue

Brown acrylic paint

Three 16-inch [41-cm] lengths of 20-gauge straight floral wire

Vessel prepared with foam

Gravel or ground cover of your choice

Plant notes: This plant is composed of approximately 10 leaves in two sizes, a crown, 3 baby leaves, and aerial roots, all in a 4-inch-diameter [10-cm] pot. The approximate finished size is 13 inches high × 16 inches wide [33 × 41 cm].

STEP 1

CONNECT THE WIRE AND PAPER.

Reserve the sheet of ochre-green and one sheet of dark green paper to make baby leaves. Wrap ten 16-inch [41-cm] 18-gauge wires with orange floral tape, covering the wire completely. Mock up the template placement for 5 each of the large and small leaves on the dark green paper (fitting 2 leaves per sheet) and mark with a pencil where the wrapped wires will be placed. Make paper-and-wire sandwiches by following the instructions on page 45 for the double-sided adhesive method. Secure the wires in place by pressing the bone folder around the contours of each wire.

STEP 2

TRACE AND CUT OUT THE LEAVES.

Position the 2 templates over the wires in the paper-and-wire sandwiches, making sure the wires protrude from the crevice in the base (not the pointy end) of the leaf shapes. Trace approximately 5 each of the large and small leaf shapes and use scissors (or an X-Acto knife) to cut them out. If necessary, use an X-Acto knife to carefully cut around the wire at the base of the leaf to release the paper that is adhered to the stem.

STEP 3

ADD DETAILS TO THE LEAVES.

The top sides of these leaves have lime green veins, and the undersides have hot pink veins. Using the lime green gel pen, draw an elongated Y shape on one side of a leaf, starting from the pointy end of the leaf and drawing over the wire. Then draw several veins branching off perpendicularly from the Y shape. Allow the ink to dry, then flip the leaf over and draw a shorter Y shape on the back side of the leaf with the hot pink gel pen. Repeat for all the leaves.

STEP 4

CREATE A CROWN.

Following the instruction on page 55 for making a crown, create 1 small crown for this plant and insert it into the vessel prepared with foam.

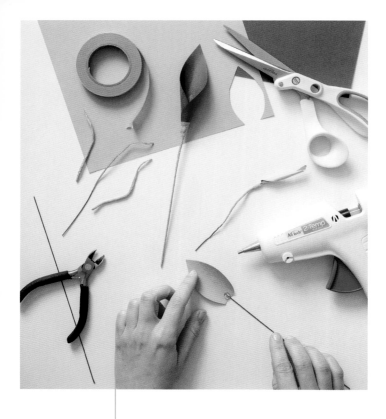

STEP 5

CRAFT BABY LEAVES AND AERIAL ROOTS.

Using the wire cutters, cut three 8-inch [20.5 cm] lengths of 16-inch [41-cm] 20-gauge wire. Following the instructions on page 59 for making baby leaves, make 1 dark green baby leaf and 2 ochre-green baby leaves. Cover the connection and the stem with orange floral tape. Next, make 3 to 5 aerial roots by cutting the remaining 20-gauge wire to five 3-inch [7.5-cm] lengths. Wrap each length with orange floral tape, and as you reach the end of the wire keep wrapping and twisting the floral tape past the end of the wire for a couple of inches, twisting it to itself.

STEP 6

SHAPE THE LEAVES.

Add shape to the leaves by bending the wire in a leaf to make a gentle curve. In one hand, hold the leaf firmly where the wire is attached. Bend the wire down with your other hand, arching the stem just above where it connects to the leaf. Repeat for all the leaves.

Assemble the plant by inserting the stems of the large leaves into the crown, being sure to pierce through the crown into the vessel prepared with foam as well. Place the leaves at slightly different curves and angles. Lastly, add the baby leaves and aerial roots to the crown. Cover the foam with ground cover.

Sassafras Seedlings

Sassafras is one of the trees that I look for while I'm hiking in Prospect Park. All the parts of this plant are fragrant! It's so satisfying to find this gem, lightly rub a leaf, and get a glorious whiff of root beer. I am also fascinated with this tree because it has three distinct leaf shapes, including one that is mitten-shaped. I love to hunt for sassafras seedlings that sprout up around a larger tree, because each seedling will often have all three leaf shapes in a vibrant fresh green.

TOOLS

Pencil

Wire cutters

Bone folder

Scissors

X-Acto knife

MATERIALS

6 templates (page 257)

2 sheets of 8½- × 11-inch [21.5- × 28-cm] medium green text-weight paper

Six 16-inch [41-cm] lengths of 20-gauge red straight floral wire

1 sheet of double-sided adhesive cut to 8½- × 11 inches [21.5 × 28 cm]

Lime green gel pen

Green floral tape

3 vessels prepared with foam

Gravel or ground cover of your choice

Plant notes: Each seedling is composed of 4 or 5 leaves. I suggest making several of each leaf size and shape, then compose your seedling with a combination of leaves to your liking. All are planted in 2-inch-diameter [5-cm] pots. The approximate finished size is 7 inches high × 8 inches wide [18 × 20.5 cm].

STEP 1

CONNECT THE WIRE AND PAPER.

Because you are making small leaves, cut the paper and double-sided sheets in half so you have strips measuring 4¼ × 11 inches [11 × 28 cm]. Mock up the template placement for approximately 18 leaves in the various sizes (fitting 8 to 10 leaves per strip) and mark with a pencil where the wires will be placed. Because the sizes of the leaf shapes are so varied, fully trace the leaves to more easily place your wires if you like. Using wire cutters, cut the wires into 18 lengths approximately 5 inches [13 cm] long. Make paper-and-wire sandwiches by following the instructions on page 45 for the double-sided adhesive method. Secure the wires in place by pressing the bone folder around the contours of each wire.

STEP 2

TRACE AND CUT OUT THE LEAVES.

Position the 6 templates over the wires in the paper-and-wire sandwiches, making sure the wires protrude from the center of the base of the leaf shapes. Trace approximately 18 leaf shapes in the various sizes and shapes and use scissors (or an X-Acto knife) to cut them out.

STEP 3

ADD DETAILS TO THE LEAVES.

Draw veins onto each leaf with a lime green gel pen. Start by drawing a line along the wire, tapering it at the tip of the leaf, then add lines branching off either side. Draw the veins on each leaf slightly differently. Color in about 1/8‑inch [3 mm] of the top of the red stem wire just below the leaf with the lime green ink as well. Add gel pen details to both sides of each leaf and stem.

STEP 4

CONNECT THE STEMS TO MAKE SEEDLINGS.

Connect 2 stems together to start a seedling. Start wrapping floral tape around the 2 stems about 1 to 1½ inches [2.5 to 4 cm] below the base of the leaves, so that some of the red wire stem remains exposed. Add a third leaf, also leaving about 1 to 1½ inches [2.5 to 4 cm] of the red wire stem exposed. Evaluate your seedling. Does it need more leaves? If so, add 1 or 2 more, choosing the shapes and sizes that look good to you. Repeat to make 3 seedlings. Next, separate the wires where they're not covered with floral tape, bending them so that the leaves spray out. Gently bend the wire inside some of the leaves to give them a curve.

Insert the stems into the vessel prepared with foam. Cover the foam with ground cover.

Alocasia infernalis

Alocasia infernalis is a stellar species of elephant ear. It's distinctive for its deep purplish blue-black—dare I say sexy?—leaves. The stems are black as well, with new growth emerging as green and darkening with age. My next apartment will be all jewel tones and dark saturated colors, and I'll make one of these to sit next to my red velvet couch. I'll say things like "Welcome to my boudoir" whenever friends visit!

TOOLS

Palette

Large spray bottle with water

1-inch [2.5-cm] flat paintbrush

Pencil

Scissors

X-Acto knife

Wire cutters

Bone folder

MATERIALS

3 templates (pages 264, 265)

Dark blue and pale green acrylic paints

11 sheets of 8½- × 11-inch [21.5- × 28-cm] maroon text-weight paper

6 sheets of double-sided adhesive cut to 8½ × 11 inches [21.5 × 28 cm]

Twelve 16-inch [41-cm] lengths of 18-gauge black straight floral wire

Hot pink gel pen

Vessel prepared with foam

Gravel or ground cover of your choice

Plant notes: This plant is composed of 10 leaves—5 large and 5 small—and 3 new-growth blades, all in a 5-inch-diameter [13-cm] basket. The approximate finished size is 22 inches high × 22 inches wide [56 × 56 cm].

STEP 1

PREPARE THE PAPER.

Following the instructions on page 36 for making a wash, paint a wash of dark blue acrylic paint on one side of each sheet of maroon paper. Allow the paper to dry fully. Next, orient one sheet of blue-painted paper horizontally and paint a pale green stripe along the bottom edge.

STEP 2

CONNECT THE WIRE AND PAPER.

Reserve the paper with the green stripe for making new-growth blades. Using the remaining sheets of painted paper, mock up the template placement for 5 each of the large and small leaves on the unpainted side of the paper (fitting 2 leaves per sheet) and mark with a pencil where the 16-inch [41-cm] wires will be placed. Make paper-and-wire sandwiches (painted side facing out) by following the instructions for the double-sided adhesive method on page 45. Secure the wires in place by pressing the bone folder around the contours of each wire.

STEP 3

TRACE AND CUT OUT THE LEAVES.

Position the 2 leaf templates over the wires in the paper-and-wire sandwiches, making sure the wires protrude from the crevice in the base (not the pointy end) of the leaf shapes. Trace approximately 5 each of the large and small leaf shapes and use scissors (or an X-Acto knife) to cut them out. If necessary, use an X-Acto knife to carefully cut around the wire at the base of the leaf to release the paper that is adhered to the stem.

STEP 4

ADD DETAILS TO THE LEAVES.

Using the hot pink gel pen, draw a heavy line on each leaf along the wire. Start at the base of the leaf, and allow the line to taper off as you get closer to the tip.

STEP 5

FOLD THE LEAVES.

Fold each leaf in half lengthwise along the wire. With a leaf still folded, gently press several creases along the leaf at a 45-degree angle from the stem. Make the creases about 1 to 1¹/₂ inches [2.5 to 4 cm] apart. Open the leaf and gently flatten it out, allowing the creases to remain as the veins. Repeat for all the leaves.

STEP 6

CREATE THE NEW-GROWTH BLADES.

Position the reserved sheet of paper horizontally with the green stripe at the bottom and cut the paper in half to make 2 pieces measuring 5¹/₂ × 8¹/₂ inches [14 × 21.5 cm] inches. Cut a sheet of double-sided adhesive in half the same way; you'll only need half the sheet for this step. Mock up the template placement for 3 new-growth blades on the unpainted side of the paper and mark with a pencil where the wires will be placed, making sure the painted stripe is at the base (not the pointy end) of the blade shape and facing out. Using wire cutters, cut the remaining wires into 3 lengths approximately 8 inches [20.5 cm] long. Make a paper-and-wire sandwich by following the instructions for the double-sided adhesive method on page 45. Secure the wires in place by pressing the bone folder around the contours of each wire. Use scissors to cut out the blades.

Assemble the plant by first inserting the leaf stems into the vessel prepared with foam, placing all stems close together in the center of the pot. Then, insert the new-growth blades around the stems of the leaves, inserting the wire all the way to the base of the blade. Gently bend some the leaves down to create nuance. Cover the foam with ground cover.

Christmas Cactus

Zygocactus, more widely and affectionately known as the Christmas cactus, is a bit wild and wonderful, with curvy and jaunty stems. Made with vibrant red and green paper, it's a great gift for the holidays. Not surprisingly, *Zygocactus* blooms around Christmastime with large red, pink, or orange flowers. You can make a full-size plant, like the one shown here, or you can easily make a smaller version with only two or three stems. How fun would this paper plant be as a party favor or place card at your next holiday get-together?

TOOLS

Pencil

Bone folder

X-Acto knife

Scissors

Wire cutters

MATERIALS

3 templates (page 283)

12 sheets of 8½- × 11-inch [21.5- × 28-cm] medium green text-weight paper

6 sheets of double-sided adhesive cut to 8½ × 11 inches [21.5 × 28 cm]

Twenty-five 16-inch [41-cm] lengths of 20-gauge green straight floral wire

Red tissue paper

Paste glue

Green floral tape

Vessel prepared with foam

Gravel or ground cover of your choice

Plant notes: This plant is unique as it is the only one in the book that has flowers. The flowers add to the character and spirit of the plant. The plant is composed of approximately 25 leaves in three sizes and 3 to 5 flowers in a 5-inch-diameter [13-cm] pot. The approximate finished size is 11 inches high × 14 inches wide [28 × 35.5 cm].

STEP 1

CONNECT THE WIRE AND PAPER.

Reserve 2 sheets of green paper to make the leaves with flowers. Using the remaining sheets of green paper, mock up the template placement for approximately 20 leaves in various sizes (fitting 4 to 6 leaves per sheet). Mark with a pencil where the 16-inch [41-cm] wires will be placed (the wire should extend nearly the full length of the leaf shape and can be cut down later if need be). Make paper-and-wire sandwiches by following the instructions on page 45 for the double-sided adhesive method. Secure the wires in place by pressing the bone folder around the contours of each wire.

STEP 2

TRACE AND CUT OUT THE LEAVES.

Position the 3 templates over the wires in the paper-and-wire sandwiches, making sure the wires protrude from the center of the base (not the pointy end) of the leaf shapes. Trace approximately 20 leaf shapes in various sizes and use an X-Acto knife to cut them out.

STEP 3

CUT THE TISSUE PAPER
FOR THE FLOWERS.

Cut a piece of tissue paper to approximately
2¹/₂ × 8 inches [6.5 × 20.5 cm]. Fold the tissue
paper in half and in half again. Keep folding
the paper in half until it is about ¹/₂ inch
[12 mm] wide. Using scissors, cut one end of
the folded paper to a point. Repeat to make
3 to 5 flowers.

STEP 4

ASSEMBLE THE FLOWERS.

Unfold and flatten out the cut pieces of tissue
paper, then apply a line of paste glue along
the straight edge. Wrap a piece of tissue paper
around the end of a wire, occasionally pinching
the tissue to create dimension. Once the paper
is completely wrapped around the wire, cover
the connection with green floral tape. Repeat
for all the flowers.

STEP 5

CONNECT THE FLOWERS AND PAPER.

Mock up the template placement and note where to place the wires before you start working with the adhesive. Position the stems so that the flower and about 1/2 inch [12 mm] of the stem protrude above the edge of the paper. The leaves with the flowers I've made here are short, but if you'd like long leaves with flowers, position the paper vertically and use the longer template and longer wires. Connect the wire and paper following the directions on page 45 for the double-sided adhesive method.

STEP 6

SECURE THE WIRES AND TRACE AND CUT OUT THE LEAVES.

Secure the wires in place by running your bone folder around all the contours of the wires. Position the templates over the wires in the paper-and-wire sandwich, making sure the wire protrudes from the center of the base of the leaf shapes (the rounded end without sharp points). Trace the templates and cut out the leaves using an X-Acto knife.

Assemble the plant by inserting each stem into the vessel prepared with foam, arranging them so that they curve at different directions and angles. Cover the foam with ground cover.

Rex Begonia Vine

The rex begonia vine, also known as painted cissus, is not actually a begonia at all, but a member of the grape family. Rex thrives in warmer climates and is typically found outdoors, climbing trellises and arbors, or trailing down from hanging baskets. You can bring this showy plant indoors with a painted paper version! Create interest and realism by making leaves in various sizes and styling it so that the leaves lean toward the light.

TOOLS

Large spray bottle with water

Palette

1-inch [2.5-cm] flat and small round paintbrushes

Pencil

Wire cutters

Bone folder

Scissors

X-Acto knife

MATERIALS

3 templates (page 252)

6 sheets of 8½- × 11-inch [21.5- × 28-cm] dark green text-weight paper

Purple acrylic paint

6 sheets of 8½- × 11-inch [21.5- × 28-cm] maroon text-weight paper

Sixteen 16-inch [41-cm] lengths of 20-gauge red straight floral wires

6 sheets of double-sided adhesive cut to 8½ × 11 inches [21.5 × 28 cm]

White and green gouache paints

Violet gel pen

Red floral tape

Vessel prepared with foam

Gravel or ground cover of your choice

Plant notes: This plant is composed of approximately 36 leaves in three sizes. It consists of 2 vines of various lengths with 6 to 9 leaves each and 5 sprigs with 3 to 4 leaves each, all in a 4-inch-diameter [10-cm] pot. The approximate finished size is 18 inches high × 12 inches wide [46 × 30.5 cm].

STEP 1

PREPARE THE PAPER.

Orient a sheet of dark green paper horizontally and mist it with water. Working quickly while the paper is damp, use a 1-inch [2.5-cm] flat brush to paint 3 vertical stripes on the paper with purple acrylic paint. Paint 1 stripe in the middle and 2 more about 2 inches [5 cm] from each end of the paper. Repeat for each sheet of dark green paper. Allow the paper to dry fully. Leave the maroon paper unpainted.

STEP 2

CONNECT THE WIRE AND PAPER.

Mock up the template placement for approximately 36 leaves of various sizes on the maroon paper (fitting 6 leaves per sheet) and mark with a pencil where the wires will be placed, making sure the wires will be parallel to the painted stripes on the green paper. Using wire cutters, cut 12 of the wires into 36 lengths approximately 5 inches [13 cm] long. Make paper-and-wire sandwiches with the maroon and painted paper (painted side facing out) by following the instructions on page 45 for the double-sided adhesive method. Secure the wires in place by pressing the bone folder around the contours of each wire.

STEP 3

TRACE AND CUT OUT THE LEAVES.

Position the 3 templates over the wires in the paper-and-wire sandwiches, making sure the wire protrudes from the crevice in the base (not the pointy end) of the leaf shapes. Trace approximately 36 leaf shapes in various sizes and use scissors (or an X-Acto knife) to cut them out. If necessary, use an X-Acto knife to carefully cut around the wire at the base of the leaf to release the paper that is adhered to the stem.

STEP 4

ADD DETAILS TO THE LEAVES.

Mix green and white gouache paint to create a pale green color and lightly dilute the paint with water. Using the pattern for painting on page 286 as a guide, paint decorative dots and teardrop shapes on each leaf with a small round paintbrush. Allow the paint to dry fully. To create veins, use a violet gel pen to draw a line down the center and between the larger teardrop shapes.

STEP 5

CONNECT THE STEMS TO MAKE VINES AND SPRIGS.

Create a vine with a 20-gauge 16-inch [41-cm] wire. Using red floral tape, wrap the stem of 1 small leaf to the end of the wire 1 to 2 inches [2.5 to 5 cm] from the base of the leaf. Continue to attach leaf stems to the wire, one at a time, at approximately 2-inch [5-cm] intervals as you work down the length of the wire. Alternate randomly between attaching large and medium leaves until you have attached approximately 10 leaves. Using wire cutters, cut a length of 20-gauge wire to 12 inches [30.5 cm] long and repeat these steps to create a vine with approximately 6 leaves. Then, cut five 5-inch [13-cm] lengths of 20-gauge wire and, still using red floral tape, wrap 3 to 4 leaves to each length to create 5 sprigs.

STEP 6

STYLE THE VINES AND SPRIGS.

Bend each leaf to alternating sides of the vine, occasionally pulling a leaf toward you to stage each leaf a little differently.

Assemble the plant by inserting the longer vines on one side of the vessel prepared with foam and filling in with the shorter sprigs. Cover the foam with ground cover.

Peruvian Maidenhair Fern

I first became aware of maidenhair ferns when I was hiking redwood forests in California, and I came upon a small stream set between two steep rock faces. Every inch of vertical surface was covered in dripping, vibrant, fluttering maidenhair ferns. Ever since then, they've held a soft spot in my heart. There is a beautiful example of the Peruvian maidenhair fern in the conservatory at the Brooklyn Botanic Garden. They have strikingly large and varied leaf shapes on arching fronds. The leaves have a straight edge that makes them look as if they have been folded along the black stem, which is what we will be doing here with a slight modification to the double-sided adhesive method.

TOOLS

Pencil

Scissors

X-Acto knife

Bone folder

Wire cutters

MATERIALS

6 templates (page 282)

12 sheets of double-sided adhesive cut to 8½ × 11 inches [21.5 × 28 cm]

12 sheets of 8½- × 11-inch [21.5- × 28-cm] light green text-weight paper

24-gauge spool wire

Black floral tape

Twelve 16-inch [41-cm] lengths of 18-gauge black straight floral wire

Vessel prepared with foam

Gravel or ground cover of your choice

Plant notes: This plant is composed of 132 leaves in six shapes to make 12 fronds in a 6-inch-diameter [15-cm] pot. The approximate finished size is 17 inches high × 23 inches wide [43 × 58.5 cm].

STEP 1

ATTACH THE DOUBLE-SIDED ADHESIVE.

Attach a sheet of double-sided adhesive to the light green paper, leaving 1 side of the white protective paper in place.

STEP 2

TRACE AND CUT OUT THE LEAVES.

Keep the protective paper in place on each sheet of light green paper. For every frond, you need 1 leaf shape of the smallest template and 2 leaf shapes each of the other 5 templates for a total of 132 leaves. Use the small template to trace 12 of the smallest leaf shapes. Use the other 5 templates to trace 24 of each leaf shape. Use scissors (or an X-Acto knife) to cut out the leaves.

STEP 3

FOLD THE LEAVES.

With the protective paper still in place, fold
each leaf in half, matching up the edges and
using a bone folder to press the crease. Repeat
for all the leaves.

STEP 4

CONNECT THE WIRE TO THE LEAVES.

Use wire cutters to cut 132 lengths of 24-gauge
spool wire at approximately 4 inches [10 cm]
long. Wrap each 4-inch [10 cm] piece with black
floral tape. One at a time, peel the protective
paper off a leaf and place a wrapped wire in
the crease overlapping the leaf by about 1 inch
[2.5 cm]. Fold the leaf around the wire, adher-
ing the sticky sides together, matching up the
edges. Use a bone folder to press around the
contours of the wire. Repeat for all the leaves.

STEP 5

CONNECT THE STEMS TO MAKE FRONDS.

Create a frond with an 18-gauge 16-inch [41-cm] wire. Using black floral tape, wrap the stem of 1 small leaf to the end of the wire about 1 inch [2.5 cm] from the base of the leaf. Continue to attach leaf stems to the wire, one at a time, at approximately 1-inch [2.5-cm] intervals, alternating sides as you work down the length of the wire. Add the smaller leaves first until you have attached approximately 11 leaves. Repeat these steps to create 12 fronds.

STEP 6

CONNECT THE FRONDS.

For added realism, attach 2 fronds together using black floral tape. For this plant, I made 2 pairs of double fronds, and left the rest as singles.

Insert the stems into the vessel prepared with foam, adding a slight curve to some of the wires and allowing the leaves to fall at different angles. Cover the foam with ground cover.

Sweet Potato Vine

The sweet potato vine, with its colorful foliage in shades of green, purple, or mauve, is an annual typically planted outdoors in early spring or summer. But if you're like me, and you'd like a pop of vibrant green in the middle of January, make a paper version! I am particularly taken with the variety I see in the planters near my subway stop. The chartreuse leaves have pinkish tips and edges. Each leaf is slightly different in size and shape. I've made a petite trailing pot of sweet potato vine, but this vine is known to grow up to 5 feet [1.5 m] long!

TOOLS

Container for mixing paint

Small spray bottle

Pencil

Wire cutters

Scissors

X-Acto knife

Bone folder

MATERIALS

3 templates (page 258)

Hot pink acrylic paint

12 sheets of 8½- × 11-inch [21.5- × 28-cm] chartreuse text-weight paper

Seventeen 16-inch [41-cm] lengths of 20-gauge light green straight floral wire

6 sheets of double-sided adhesive cut to 8½ × 11 inches [21.5 × 28 cm]

Violet alcohol marker

Green floral tape

Vessel prepared with foam

Gravel or ground cover of your choice

Plant notes: This plant is composed of approximately 36 leaves in three sizes. It consists of 3 vines of various lengths with 6 to 9 leaves each and 4 sprigs with 4 to 5 leaves each, all in a 4½-inch-diameter [11.5-cm] pot. The approximate finished size is 16 inches high × 13 inches wide [41 × 33 cm].

STEP 1

PREPARE THE PAPER.

Following the instructions on page 38 for adding color to paper by spraying paint on it, fill a spray bottle with diluted hot pink acrylic paint. Orient a sheet of paper horizontally and spray a mist of hot pink paint across the middle of the paper. Leave the other side unpainted. Paint each sheet of paper slightly differently by varying the application with more or less paint. Allow the paper to dry fully.

STEP 2

CONNECT THE WIRE AND PAPER.

Mock up the template placement for approximately 36 leaves of various sizes on the unpainted side of the paper (fitting about 6 leaves per sheet) and mark with a pencil where the wires will be placed. Using wire cutters, cut 12 of the wires into 36 lengths approximately 5 inches [13 cm] long. Make paper-and-wire sandwiches with the painted paper (painted side facing out) by following the instructions on page 45 for the double-sided adhesive method. Secure the wires in place by pressing the bone folder around the contours of each wire.

STEP 3

TRACE AND CUT OUT THE LEAVES.

Position the 3 templates over the wires in the paper-and-wire sandwiches, making sure the wires protrude from the crevice in the base (not the pointy end) of the leaf shapes. Trace approximately 36 leaf shapes in various sizes and use scissors (or an X-Acto knife) to cut them out. If necessary, use an X-Acto knife to carefully cut around the wire at the base of the leaf to release the paper that is adhered to the stem.

STEP 4

ADD DETAILS TO THE LEAVES.

Holding a leaf at an angle, run the tip of a violet alcohol marker along the edge of a leaf. The paper will quickly absorb the ink, leaving a violet border around the leaf on the front and back sides. Repeat for at least half of the leaves.

STEP 5

CONNECT THE STEMS TO MAKE VINES AND SPRIGS.

Create a vine with a 16-inch 20-gauge [41-cm] wire. Using green floral tape, wrap the stem of 1 small leaf to the end of the wire 1 to 2 inches [2.5 to 5 cm] from the base of the leaf. Continue to attach leaf stems to the wire, one at a time, approximately every 2 inches [5 cm] as you work down the length of the wire. Alternate randomly between attaching medium and large leaves until you have attached approximately 9 leaves. Using wire cutters, cut two 12-inch [30.5-cm] lengths of 20-gauge wire and repeat these steps to create vines with 6 to 7 leaves each. Then, cut four 4- to 5-inch [10- to 13-cm] lengths of 20-gauge wire and, still using green floral tape, wrap 4 to 5 leaves to each length to create 4 sprigs.

STEP 6

STYLE THE VINES.

Gently bend each leaf to alternating sides of the vines, occasionally pulling one toward you to add variety.

Assemble the plant by inserting 1 long and 1 medium-length vine on one side of the vessel prepared with foam, and insert a single medium-length vine on the other side. Fill the rest of the pot with the shorter sprigs. If the foam is visible, cover it with ground cover.

Spiral Ginger

A real showstopper, the spiral ginger is a rare plant typically found in Indonesia. It has delicate crepe-like flowers, but it's also celebrated for its row of spirally arranged leaves. This varietal sports a thick red stem with leaves stacked on the outside edge like a spiral staircase. I am trying to convince my family to grow one; sometimes, you have to live vicariously through people with yards! Otherwise, you make one out of paper.

TOOLS

Pencil

Wire cutters

Bone folder

Scissors

Palette

Small round paintbrush

Hot-glue gun and glue sticks

MATERIALS

3 templates (pages 266, 267)

21 sheets of 8½- × 11-inch [21.5- × 28-cm] medium green text-weight paper

1 sheet of 8½- × 11-inch [21.5- × 28-cm] red text-weight paper

10 sheets of double-sided adhesive cut to 8½ × 11 inches [21.5 × 28 cm]

White and green gouache paints

Fifteen 16-inch [41-cm] lengths of 20-gauge red straight floral wire

White glue

³⁄₁₆-inch [5-mm] armature wire

Red floral tape

Vessel prepared with two layers of foam

Gravel or ground cover of your choice

Plant notes: This plant is composed of approximately 28 leaves in three sizes on 1 length of armature wire, a baby leaf, and a sprout in a 8-inch-diameter [20.5-cm] pot. The approximate finished size is 22 inches high × 24 inches wide [56 × 61 cm].

STEP 1

CONNECT THE WIRE AND PAPER.

Reserve 1 sheet of medium green paper and the 1 sheet of red paper to make baby leaves and sprouts. Using the remaining medium green sheets of paper, mock up the template placement for approximately 28 leaves of various sizes (fitting 3 to 4 leaves per sheet) and mark with a pencil where the wires will be placed. Using wire cutters, cut 14 of the 20-gauge wires into 28 lengths approximately 8 inches [20.5 cm] long. Make paper-and-wire sandwiches by following the instructions on page 45 for the double-sided adhesive method. Secure the wires in place by pressing the bone folder around the contours of each wire.

STEP 2

TRACE AND CUT OUT THE LEAVES.

Position the 3 templates over the wires in the paper-and-wire sandwiches, making sure the wires protrude from one point of the leaf shapes. Trace approximately 28 leaf shapes in various sizes and use scissors to cut them out.

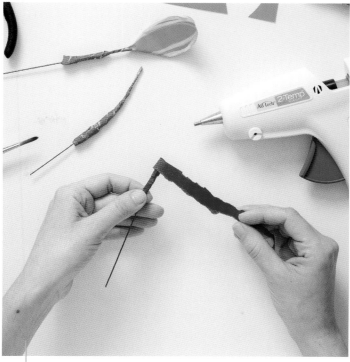

STEP 3

ADD DETAILS TO THE LEAVES.

Mix green and white gouache paint to create a pale green color and lightly dilute the paint with water. Using a small round paintbrush, paint long, loose strokes along the edges of each leaf. Once dry, paint the same loose strokes on the other side. Differ the pattern from leaf to leaf by painting fewer or more strokes along all the edges.

STEP 4

CRAFT A BABY LEAF AND A SPROUT.

Cut a small leaf out of the remaining sheet of green paper and paint the edges, following the instructions for painting in step 3. Following the instructions on page 59 for making baby leaves, make a baby leaf on a 5-inch [13-cm] length of 20-gauge wire. Tear several strips of red paper at about 1/2 inch [12 mm] wide. Wrap the base and about half of the stem of the baby leaf with a torn red strip of paper and secure it with white glue. To make a sprout, wrap a piece of wire cut to about 4 inches [10 cm] with a strip of torn red paper and secure it with white (or hot) glue. Next, using white gouache paint, paint a few small dots on the red-paper accents.

STEP 5

CONNECT THE STEMS.

Straighten a length of armature wire to create a main stem. Using red floral tape, connect the stems of 3 small or medium leaves together. Then, attach the 3 leaves to the end of the armature wire with red floral tape flush with the base of the leaves. Wrap the remaining leaves to one side of the armature wire about 1 inch [2.5 cm] apart, working with 1 leaf at a time, placing the base of the leaf flush against the armature wire as you work down the length of the main stem. Once you have attached all the leaves, cut the armature wire at about 12 inches [30.5 cm] below the last leaf and wrap the last 12 inches [30.5 cm] with red floral tape. Attach a strip of torn red paper at about 3 inches [7.5 cm] above the end of the armature wire and add white gouache paint dots. This spot will ultimately be flush with the ground cover.

STEP 6

STYLE THE PLANT.

Handling the wire and leaves carefully, shape the plant into a spiral by curving the wire bit by bit. You can shape it into a low wide spiral like the plant shown here, or into a tight tall spiral. Get the shape as close to your liking as you can before you insert the end of the armature wire into the vessel prepared with foam. When you are happy with the placement, insert the sprouts and baby leaf into the foam as well. Cover the foam with ground cover.

Oxalis

Mother Nature has gifted us with more than 800 varieties of *Oxalis*, in nearly every color, shape, and size imaginable. Some are even edible! I've combined my two favorites here, using the shape of *Oxalis triangularis* and the coloring of *Oxalis tetraphylla*. This project is unique in how the wire and leaves are connected, but I think you will find it is easy to do. The end result is quite fragile, so keep away any swatting cats!

TOOLS

Pencil

Scissors

X-Acto knife

Cotton swabs

Containers for glue and isopropyl alcohol

Bone folder

Wire cutters

¼-inch [6-mm] flat paintbrush for applying glue

MATERIALS

1 template (page 262)

3 sheets of 8½- × 11-inch [21.5- × 28-cm] medium green text-weight paper

Purple alcohol marker

Isopropyl alcohol

White glue

Six 16-inch [41-cm] lengths of 20-gauge green straight floral wire

Green floral tape

Vessel prepared with foam

Gravel or ground cover of your choice

Plant notes: This plant is composed of 36 leaves on 12 stems in a 4-inch-diameter [10-cm] pot. The approximate finished size is 8 inches high × 10 inches wide [20.5 × 25.5 cm].

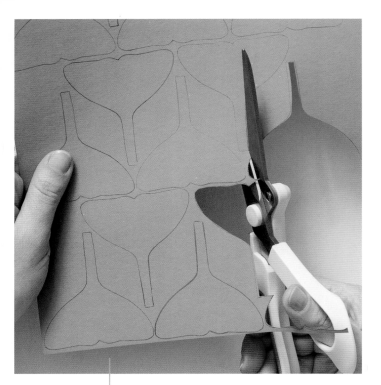

STEP 1

TRACE AND CUT OUT THE LEAVES.

Use the template to trace the leaf shape onto the paper, fitting as many as you can on each sheet. Trace 36 leaf shapes, then use scissors (or an X-Acto knife) to cut out the leaves.

STEP 2

ADD DETAILS TO THE LEAVES.

Using the purple alcohol marker, color in a small area of the base of a leaf. Dab the colored-in area with a cotton swab soaked in isopropyl alcohol to bleed the ink. Repeat for all the leaves.

STEP 3

FOLD THE LEAVES.

Fold each leaf in half, lining up the edges and left and right corners. Use a bone folder to press each crease.

STEP 4

CONNECT THE WIRE.

Using a wire cutter, cut the wire to approximately 8-inches [20.5-cm] long. Next, apply a layer of white glue to the paper tab on one of the leaves. Place a wire in the center of the glue and tab, with the top of the wire ending just below where the leaf shape begins to widen. Wait a few seconds, and when the glue begins to get tacky, pick up the leaf and wire and press the tab around the wire, molding it around the wire. Add a second leaf about 1/3 of the way around the wire and a third leaf in between the first 2. The 3 leaves should be glued at an equal distance around the wire. Repeat for the remaining leaves and wires.

STEP 5

COVER THE CONNECTION.

Starting just below the triangular leaf shape, wrap green floral tape tightly around the paper tabs, covering them and continuing to wrap the remainder of the wire stem. Repeat for all the stems.

STEP 6

SHAPE THE STEMS.

Add a gentle curve to the stems by carefully bending the wire. Assemble the plant by inserting the stems into the vessel prepared with foam, allowing the leaves to sit at varied angles and the stems to curve in different directions. As you assemble your plant, cut a few the wires to make shorter stems if you like. Cover the foam with ground cover.

Monstera deliciosa

If there ever was a plant that could command a room, it's *Monstera deliciosa*. A popular houseplant since the mid-eighteenth century, it boasts large fenestrate leaves that have been featured extensively in art and design. *Monstera deliciosa*. has aerial roots and an oddly shaped fruit, with scale-like skin that tastes like the perfect blend of banana and pineapple! The version I created for this book is large, at about 4 feet [1.2 m] across. You can go big, like I did, or scale it down to suit your space. That's the fun of making plants from paper—you can design them however you like!

TOOLS

Pencil

Scissors

X-Acto knife

Wire cutters

Needle-nose pliers

Hot-glue gun and glue sticks

Clippers

Small round paintbrush

Container for glue

Palette

MATERIALS

5 templates (pages 274–276)

3 to 6 sheets of oversize (at least 24 × 18 inches [61 × 46 cm]) dark green cover-weight paper

³⁄₁₆-inch [5-mm] armature wire

1-inch [2.5-cm] dark green floral tape

½-inch [12-mm] clear plastic tubing

Dark green tissue paper

White glue

Paste glue

Cotton swabs

Two 16-inch [41-cm] lengths of 20-gauge brown straight floral wire

Kraft paper

Foam

Brown acrylic paint

Skewers

Vessel prepared with 2 layers of foam

Gravel or ground cover of your choice

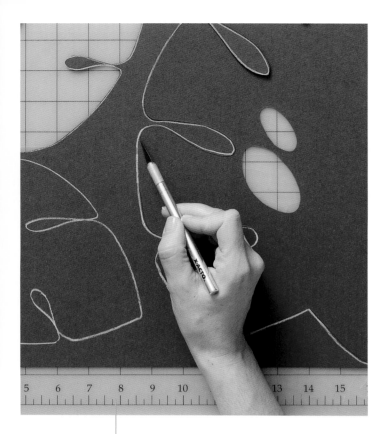

Plant notes: This plant is composed of 10 leaves—3 large, 4 medium, and 3 small—as well as a large crown and aerial roots, all in a 10-inch-diameter [25.5-cm] pot. The approximate finished size is 40 inches high × 48 inches wide [1 × 1.2 m].

STEP 1

TRACE AND CUT OUT THE LEAVES.

Use the 3 leaf-shaped templates to trace 3 large, 4 medium, and 5 small leaf shapes onto the oversize paper. Use the oval templates to trace holes in each large and medium leaf, or draw the holes freehand, being sure to avoid the centerline of the leaves. Use scissors (or an X-Acto knife) to cut out the leaves. If you like, use an X-Acto knife to lightly score a line down the center of each leaf.

STEP 2

CONNECT THE WIRE AND PAPER.

For the small leaves, straighten out a length of armature wire and use wire cutters to cut a piece about 16 inches [41 cm] long. Using needle-nose pliers, bend the wire to make a loop at one end, then bend the loop down so that it's perpendicular to the straight part of the wire. Wrap the straight part of the wire with dark green floral tape. For the medium and large leaves, straighten out a length of armature wire and cut a piece about 20 inches [51 cm] long, then make a loop as above and bend it down so that it's perpendicular to the straight part of the wire (do not cover it with floral tape). Using a dime-size amount of hot glue, secure the loop to the center of the base (not the pointy end) of each leaf. Hold it in place for several seconds as the glue hardens. Repeat for all the leaves.

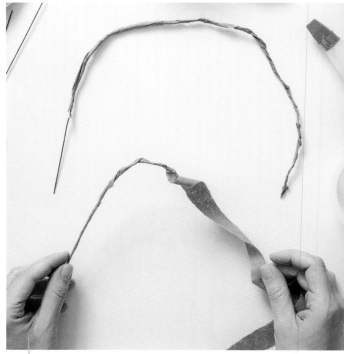

STEP 3

COVER THE CONNECTION.

For the large leaves, cut a length of plastic tubing about 6 inches [15 cm] shorter than the length of the armature wire you attached. Wrap the tubing with dark green floral tape and thread it over the armature wire attached to the leaf. Cut 3 to 5 doughnut-shaped pieces of tissue paper about 2 inches [5 cm] wide for each large leaf, and a bit smaller for the smaller leaves. Cut a slit from the edge of a doughnut-shaped piece to the center. Cover one side of the tissue paper with paste glue and wrap it around the wire and tube connection. Add 2 or 3 more pieces of tissue paper until the connection is totally covered. Repeat for all the leaves.

STEP 4

MAKE AERIAL ROOTS.

Using wire cutters, cut the 20-gauge wire into 6 lengths that are approximately 5 inches [13 cm] long. Tear several strips of kraft paper about 1/2 inch [12 mm] wide and 15 to 20 inches [38 to 51 cm] long. Cover one side of the strip with a layer of paste (or white) glue. Halfway down a 5-inch [13-cm] length of wire, start wrapping the kraft paper, allowing it to stick to the wire and to itself. Wrap and twist as you work down the wire; when you reach the end of the wire continue twisting and gluing the paper to itself until you have an approximately 12-inch [30.5-cm] long flying root. Repeat to make 5 or 6 aerial roots.

STEP 5

MAKE A CROWN.

Following the instructions on page 55 for making a crown, make a large crown, approximately 5 inches [13 cm] high, using 2 layers of foam and painting areas of dark brown acrylic paint on the kraft paper. Insert several skewers into the bottom for inserting into the vessel prepared with foam.

STEP 6

ASSEMBLE THE PLANT.

Start by inserting the crown into the vessel prepared with foam and pressing it down until the bottom of the crown is flush with the foam. Next, add 1 of the large leaves. Insert the 6-inch [15-cm] length of uncovered armature wire into the crown and through to the foam in the pot. If it is too difficult to insert, use a skewer to make a pilot hole. Insert the wire until the tube is flush with the crown. Use a piece of torn kraft paper adhered with white (or paste) glue to cover the tube-crown connection. Continue adding leaves, making sure the plant is balanced, and cover all of the connections with kraft paper. Lastly, insert the wires of your aerial roots into the crown. Cover the foam with ground cover.

Fiddle-Leaf Fig

The fiddle-leaf fig tree, or *Ficus lyrata*, is an all-time favorite among many plant enthusiasts for its whimsical appearance and large violin-shaped leaves. They remind me of something Dr. Seuss might have dreamt up. It's that fanciful quality (and the fact that I can't keep a real one alive) that inspired me to make a crafted version. This is the plant that started it all! Over the years I've made several fiddle-leafs, and these techniques have held up well. I have this paper plant in my living room, but it would also be charming in a bedroom or nursery.

TOOLS

Drill and drill bits

Clamps

Clippers

Handsaw

Bowl and whisk

1-inch [2.5-cm] flat, 1-inch [2.5-cm] chip, and a small round paintbrush

Palette

Pencil

Scissors

Bone folder

Hot-glue gun and glue sticks

MATERIALS

2 templates (pages 260, 261)

Dowels: one 1 inch [2.5 cm]; one ³⁄₁₆ inch [5 mm]; two ¼ inch [6 mm]; and two ⁵⁄₁₆ inch [7 mm]— all 48 inches [1.2 m] long

Vessel prepared with 2 layers of foam with a 1-inch-diameter [2.5-cm] hole cut in the center of the foam

Newspaper and flour

Gesso or primer

Green, brown, and yellow acrylic paints

20 sheets of 8½- × 11-inch [21.5- × 28-cm] chartreuse text-weight paper

Gravel or ground cover of your choice

Plant notes: By using bright green paint on the leaves, yellow dots on the trunk and branches, and a more whimsical shape, the fiddle-leaf fig can be a bit more stylized. Or you can make something more realistic, if you like, by toning down these aspects. This plant is composed of approximately 40 leaves on 10 branches in a 10-inch-diameter [25.5-cm] pot. The approximate finished size is 32 inches high × 34 inches wide [81 × 86 cm].

STEP 1

CONSTRUCT THE TREE.

Following the instructions on page 64 for using dowels to make a tree, construct a dowel tree in a vessel of your choice.

STEP 2

PAPIER-MÂCHÉ THE TREE.

Following the instructions on page 64 for working with papier-mâché, cover the tree with papier-mâché. Be sure to allow the papier-mâché to dry fully before moving on to the next step.

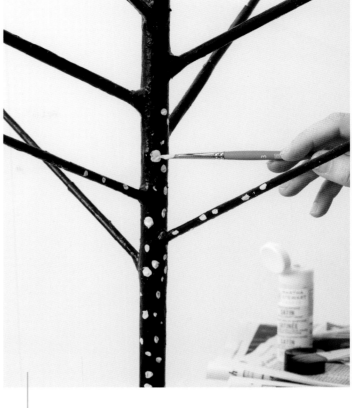

STEP 3

APPLY GESSO TO THE TREE.

Once the papier-mâché is dry, apply a layer of gesso or primer to the tree. Allow the gesso to dry fully.

STEP 4

PAINT THE TREE.

Paint the entire tree in brown acrylic paint. Once the brown paint is dry, paint yellow dots all over the tree with a small round paintbrush.

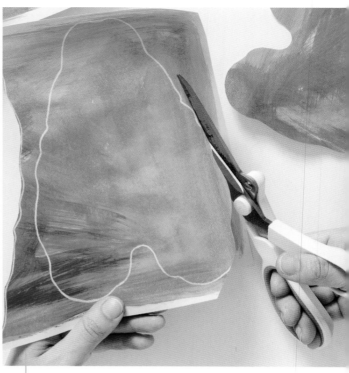

STEP 5

PREPARE THE PAPER.

Following the instructions on page 36 for the dry-brush technique, use a 1-inch [2.5-cm] chip brush to paint one side of each sheet of paper with green acrylic paint. There's no need to cover the paper completely or perfectly; a painterly application is ideal. Allow the paper to dry fully.

STEP 6

TRACE AND CUT OUT THE LEAVES.

Use the 2 templates to trace approximately 20 large and 20 small leaf shapes on the prepared paper. Use scissors to cut out the leaves.

STEP 7

FOLD THE LEAVES.

Fold each leaf in half lengthwise, with the painted side of the paper facing out, and lining up the edges. Use a bone folder to press the crease.

STEP 8

SHAPE THE LEAVES.

While the leaves are still folded in half, press several creases at a 45-degree angle along the side of each leaf. Make the folds about 1 to 1½ inches [2.5 to 4 cm] apart and use a bone folder to press each crease. Open the leaves and gently flatten them out, allowing the creases to remain as the veins.

STEP 9

CONNECT THE LEAVES.

Place 2 dots of hot glue at the base (the pointy end) of a leaf and pinch the base around the underside of a branch, holding the leaf in place where you've applied the glue. Glue each leaf at a slightly different angle, allowing some to point up or down or be horizontal on a branch. Repeat for all the leaves. Cover the foam with ground cover.

Tapioca Plant

Tapioca! Anytime I hear that word, I think of the diner scene in the film *Benny and Joon*. Joon is eating tapioca pudding and discussing the merits of raisins. At the time of the movie, I had never heard of tapioca. Now, I'm a fan, not only of the edible starch derived from the roots, but of the plant as well! The plants have uniquely shaped lobed leaves that remind me of paper snowflakes. The main stem is topped with a small umbrella of leaves, one leaf to each branch, growing up to five feet tall. I've seen potted tapioca plants in spacious modern homes, but it is certainly not limited to that aesthetic.

TOOLS

Drill and drill bits

Clamps

Handsaw

Clippers

Bowl and whisk

1-inch [2.5-cm] flat paintbrush

Palette

Pencil

Scissors

X-Acto knife

Ruler

Bone folder

MATERIALS

2 templates (pages 280, 281)

Dowels: one 1 inch [2.5 cm]; one ³⁄₁₆ inch [5 mm]; two ¼ inch [6 mm]; and two ⁵⁄₁₆ inch [7 mm]—all 48 inches [1.2 m] long

Vessel prepared with 2 layers of foam with a 1-inch-diameter [2.5-cm] hole cut in the center of the foam

Newspaper and flour

Gesso or primer

Brown acrylic paint

2 to 3 sheets of oversize (at least 24 × 18 inches [61 × 46 cm]) medium green cover-weight paper

Lime green gel pen

White glue

Gravel or ground cover of your choice

Plant notes: This plant is composed of 10 leaves, 6 small and 4 large, on 10 branches in a 12-inch-diameter [30.5-cm] pot. The approximate finished size is 44 inches high × 34 inches wide [1 m × 86 cm].

STEP 1

CONSTRUCT THE TREE.

Following the instructions on page 64 for using dowels to make a tree, construct a dowel tree in a vessel of your choice.

STEP 2

PAPIER-MÂCHÉ THE TREE.

Following the instructions on page 64 for working with papier-mâché, cover the tree with papier-mâché. Be sure to allow the papier-mâché to dry fully before moving on to the next step.

STEP 3

APPLY GESSO AND PAINT THE TREE.

Once the papier-mâché is dry, paint the tree with a layer of gesso or primer. Allow the gesso to dry fully, then paint the entire tree in brown acrylic paint

STEP 4

TRACE, CUT OUT, AND SCORE THE LEAVES.

Use the 2 templates to trace 4 large and 6 small leaf shapes on the oversize paper. Use scissors (or an X-Acto knife) to cut out the leaves. Use an X-Acto knife and a ruler to lightly score a line down the center of each lobe, and gently fold each lobe along the scored line.

ADD DETAILS TO THE LEAVES.

Make a small dot in the center of each leaf with
a lime green gel pen.

CONNECT THE LEAVES.

Use the clippers to cut the end of each branch
at a 40- to 60-degree angle; this creates a flat
surface to adhere the leaves to. Adjust the
angle until you are happy with how the leaf will
sit. Place a small dot of white glue on the cut
end of a branch and center a leaf on the glue,
with the side with the dot facing up, holding it
in place for several seconds as the glue dries.
Repeat for all the leaves. Cover the foam with
ground cover.

Bonus
Projects

One of the many joys (and delightful challenges) of crafting plants out of paper is that your creativity knows no bounds! You can increase the scale of a delicate plant. You can make pink what Mother Nature made green. You can make wreaths, hats, and even chandeliers out of paper leaves. You can spend a couple of hours on a small potted plant, or you can work for weeks to create an entire paper foliage wall. The skills you learned in the previous thirty projects can be adapted to your liking to make other plants (and use for other crafts). What follows are five projects that use the techniques you've already learned or similar ones that are easy to pick up.

Place Cards & Centerpiece

A great use for a paper plant is as a centerpiece. Here, I've used an inch plant, but you can use any plant you like. You may need to adjust the placement of the leaves and wires slightly to fit the tablescape, but this is a wonderful way to showcase your work and impress your dinner guests. To further the theme, you can make sprigs to use as place cards. Craft several small stems with three to five leaves each and simply add a paper tag with your pal's name on it to guide them to their place. Your guests can take the sprigs home as a charming party favor.

Porcelain Berry Vine Garland

The porcelain berry vine is a beautiful variegated green-and-white vine with vibrant red stems. I've created these leaves using techniques similar to those used for the sweet potato vine. White and green papers are sprayed with diluted acrylic paint to achieve the variegated look, and the vine is assembled with red floral tape. Use spool wire or simply connect lengths of straight floral wire together with red floral tape to make a longer vine. Drape the vine over a mantel as I have, or place it along a stair banister for festive holiday merriment! You can find the templates for these leaves on page 268.

Mixed Planters

One of the things I enjoy most about outdoor planters, and something that you rarely see in indoor potted plants, is mixing different plants together in one vessel. With paper plants, your combinations are based entirely on what you think works together aesthetically—there is no need to worry about soil type or sun requirements. I potted sweet potato vine, white caladium, pink and hot pink cordyline, pink polka dot, and heartleaf philodendron together in this planter. I love the contrast, color variety, and pops of pink throughout. No special tools are needed here—just prepare a large planter with foam and curate your mix!

Trellis

I can imagine this trellis as a room divider or replacing a large painting in a grand foyer. Here, I'm using a low planter box with a wooden grid trellis inserted. The planter is prepared with two layers of foam that help hold the trellis in place. I've made a crimson glory vine as it is seen in the fall, with glorious vibrant colors in shades of red, yellow, green, and maroon. To mimic the texture of changing leaves, add washes and spray the paper with acrylic paints in those hues, treating each piece of paper slightly differently. These leaves are constructed with the double-sided adhesive method, then folded in half lengthwise, then folded several times at a 45-degree angle along the side of each leaf to create the veins. There is no need to create superlong vines—if you keep the vines at 30 inches [76 cm] or shorter, they'll be easier to handle. You can create the impression of long vines by how you attach them to the trellis. The vines will stay in place if you twist them on with scraps of wire. Find the templates for the crimson glory vine on page 278.

Cloches

A glass cloche is a clever way to both visually elevate your paper plant sculptures and protect them from dust and mishaps. I created a grouping of three cloches filled with three varieties of *Oxalis*. To plant the stems in the base of a bell jar, drill holes in the base using a drill fitted with a $\frac{1}{16}$-inch [1.5-mm] bit. I recommend practicing on a scrap piece of wood before venturing on to the base itself. The hole should be the correct size to fit a 20-gauge wire covered with floral tape. The mini *Oxalis* are created using the same method as *Oxalis triangularis* described on page 214. You can create a low and bushy plant with many short stems or a lyrical statement with just a few. Find the templates for the mini *Oxalis* varieties on page 262.

Templates & Painting Patterns

Unless otherwise indicated, copy or trace the templates at the same size as they appear on these pages. If a leaf needs to be enlarged, the percentage by which it should be enlarged is noted on the page.

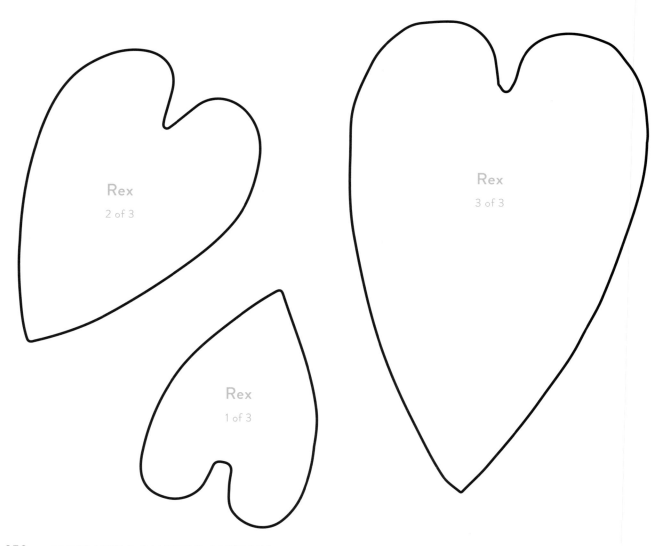

Rex
2 of 3

Rex
3 of 3

Rex
1 of 3

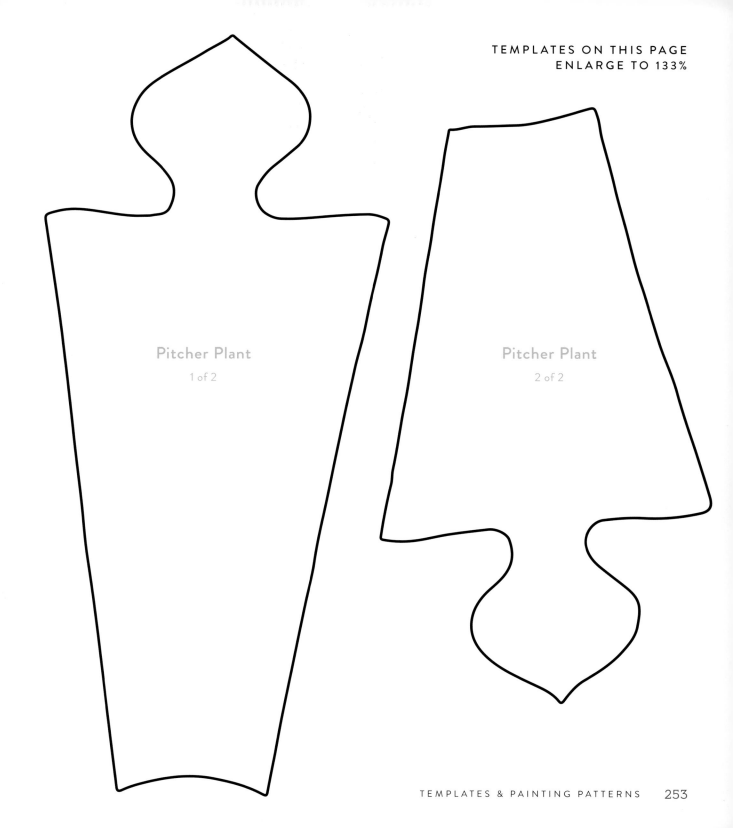

Pitcher Plant

1 of 2

Pitcher Plant

2 of 2

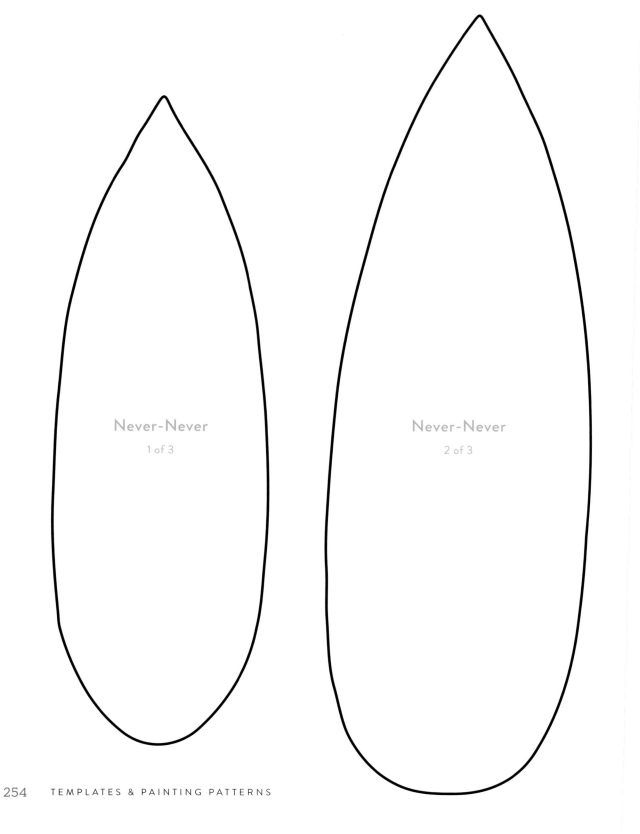

Never-Never

1 of 3

Never-Never

2 of 3

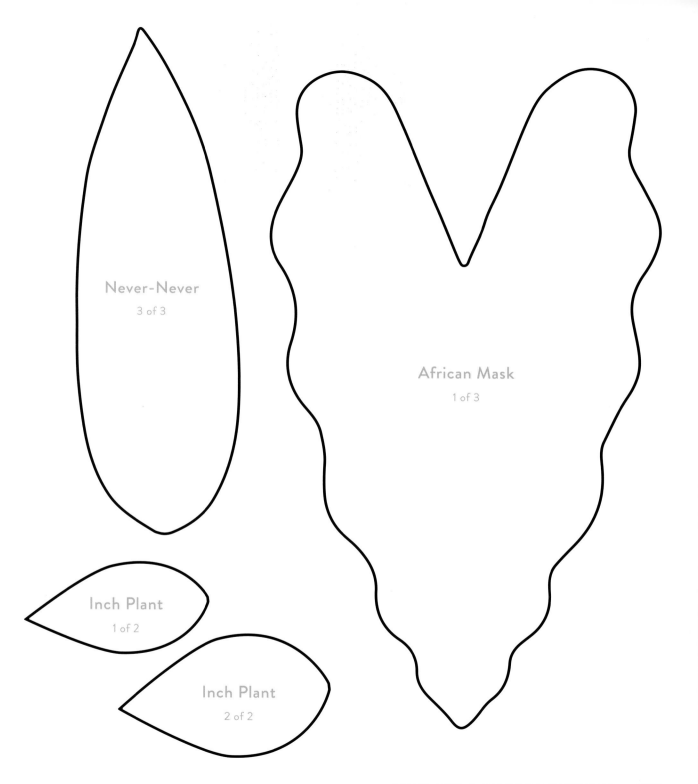

Never-Never
3 of 3

African Mask
1 of 3

Inch Plant
1 of 2

Inch Plant
2 of 2

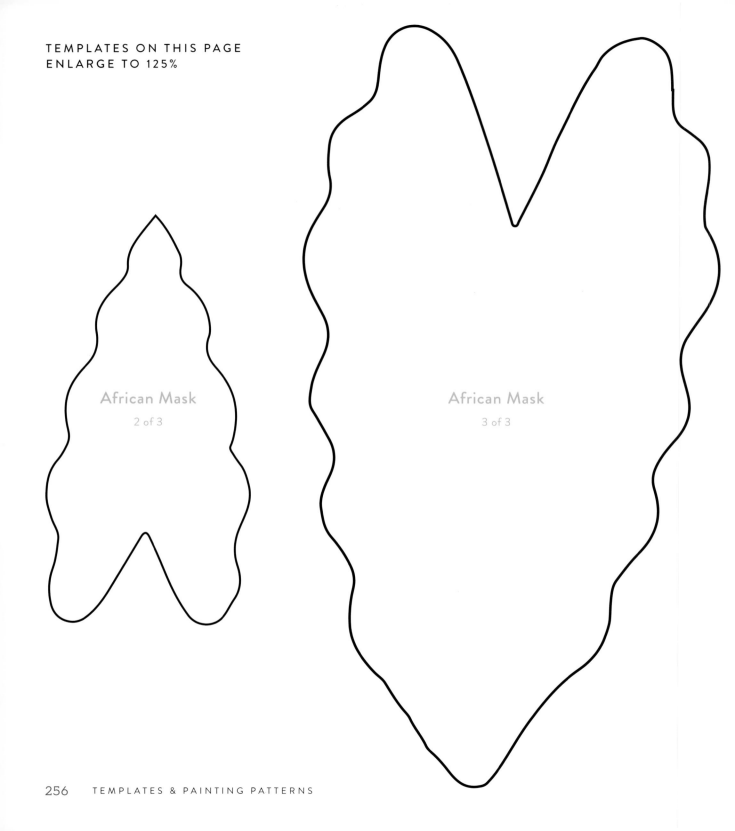

African Mask
2 of 3

African Mask
3 of 3

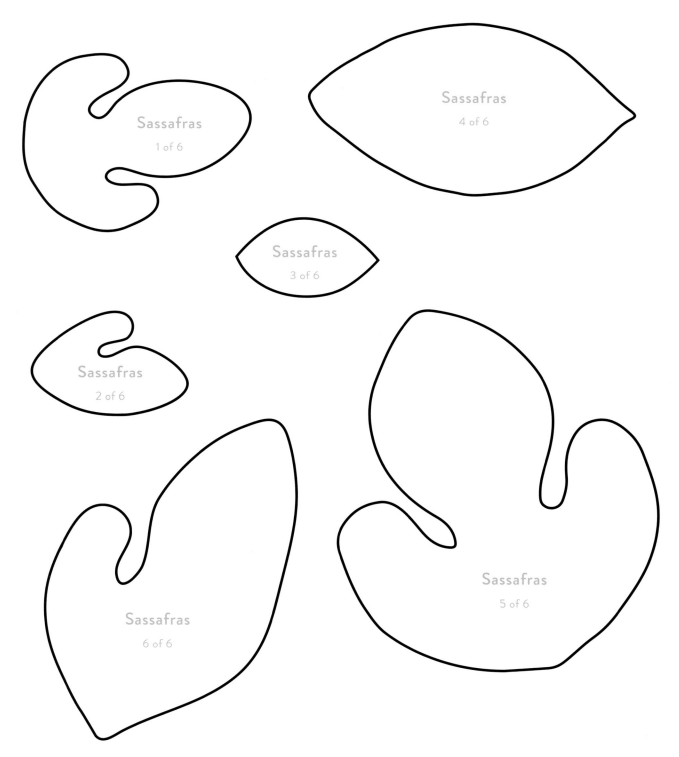

Sassafras

1 of 6

Sassafras

4 of 6

Sassafras

3 of 6

Sassafras

2 of 6

Sassafras

6 of 6

Sassafras

5 of 6

Pink Polka Dot

1 of 2

Pink
Polka Dot

2 of 2

Sweet Potato

1 of 3

Sweet Potato

3 of 3

Sweet Potato

2 of 3

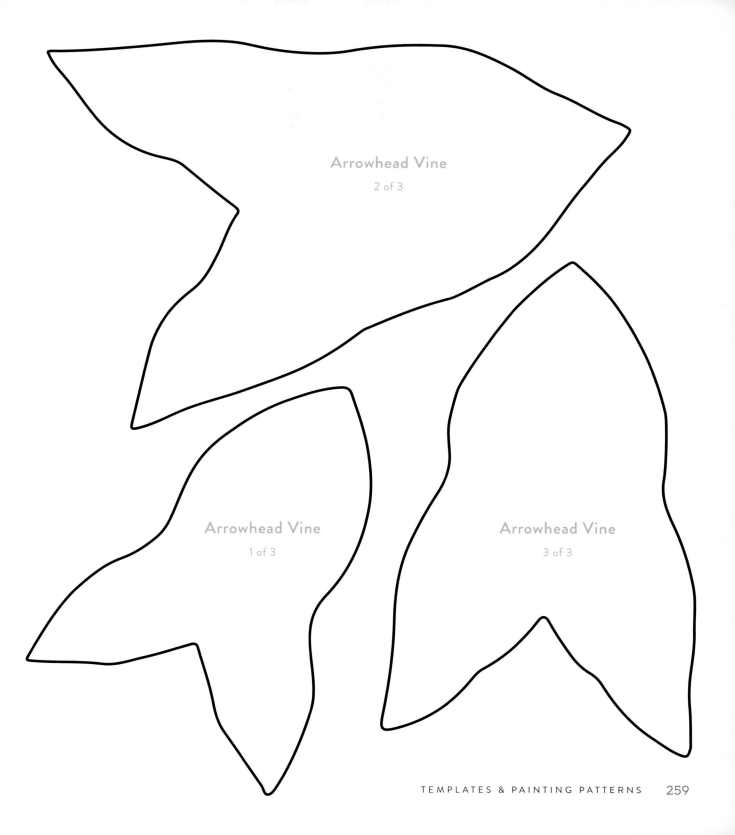

Arrowhead Vine
2 of 3

Arrowhead Vine
1 of 3

Arrowhead Vine
3 of 3

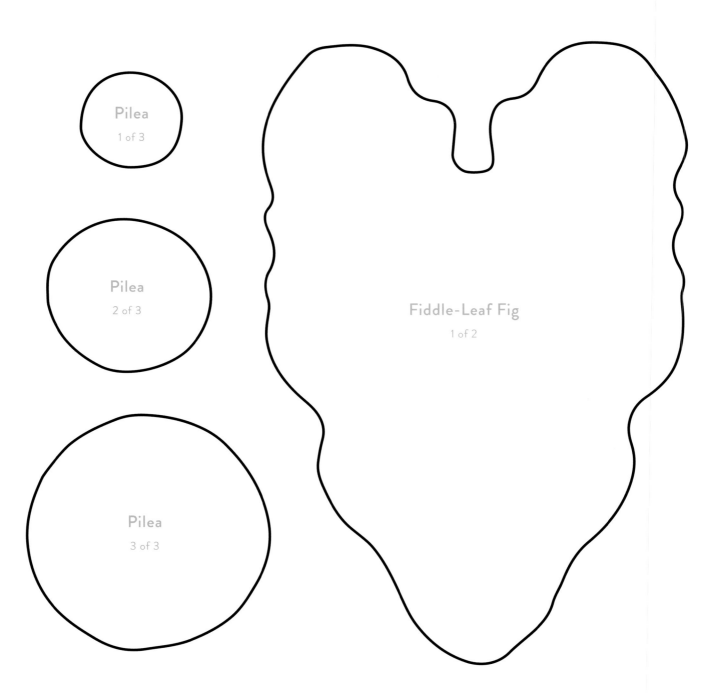

Pilea
1 of 3

Pilea
2 of 3

Pilea
3 of 3

Fiddle-Leaf Fig
1 of 2

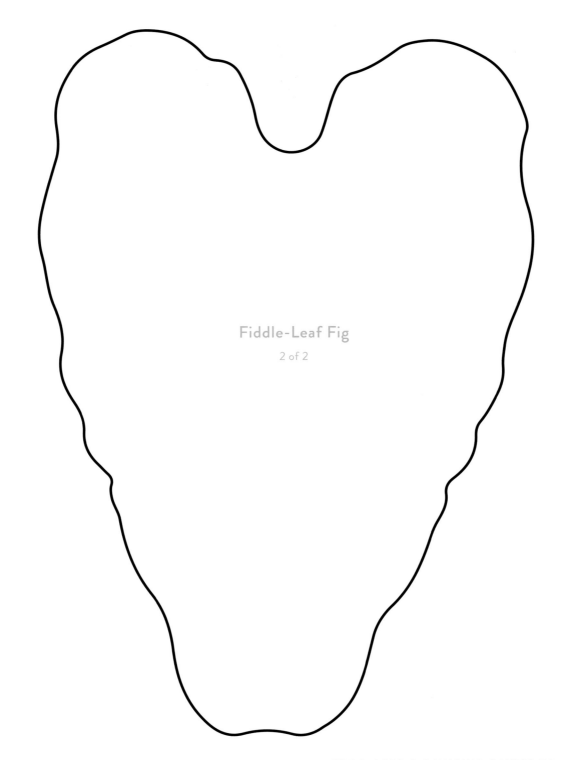

Fiddle-Leaf Fig

2 of 2

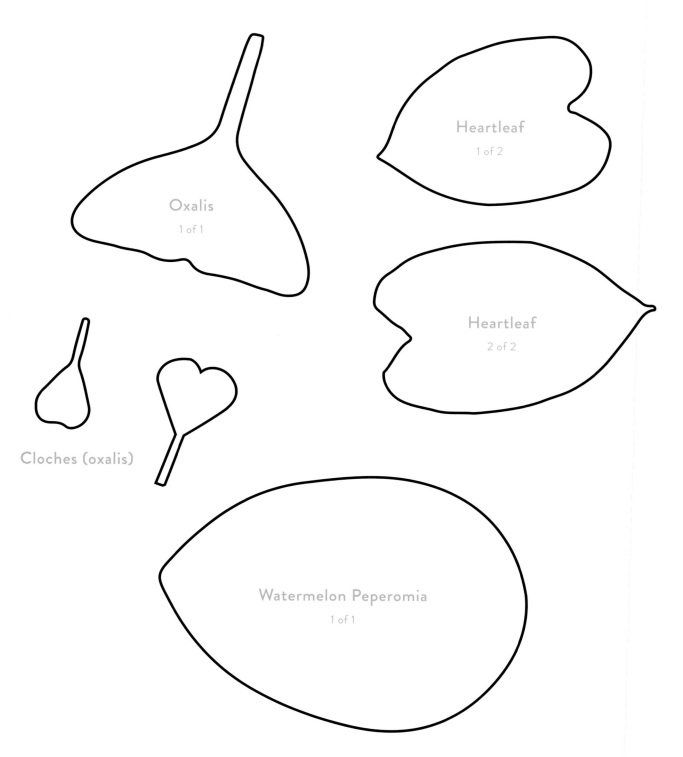

Oxalis

1 of 1

Heartleaf

1 of 2

Heartleaf

2 of 2

Cloches (oxalis)

Watermelon Peperomia

1 of 1

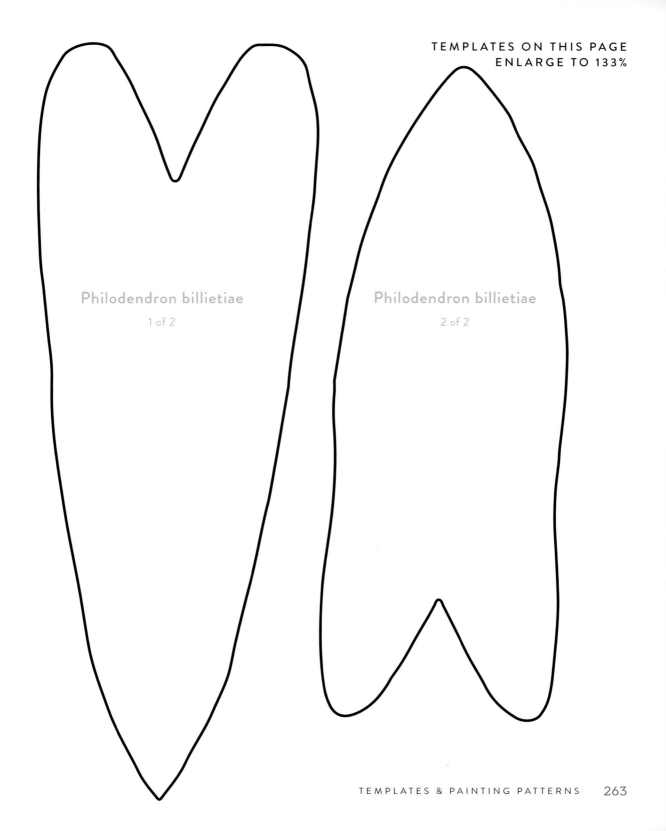

Philodendron billietiae

1 of 2

Philodendron billietiae

2 of 2

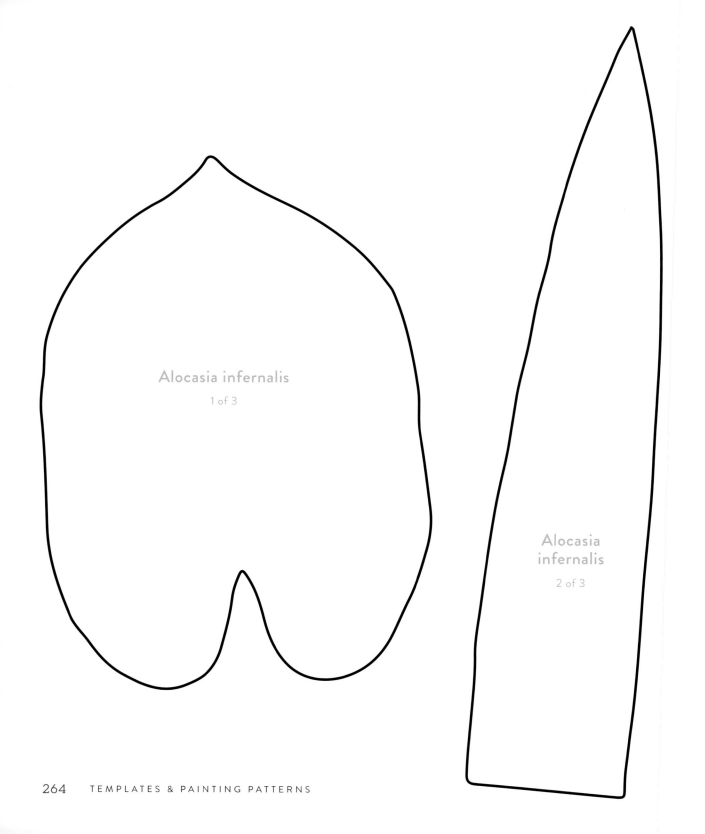

Alocasia infernalis

1 of 3

Alocasia
infernalis

2 of 3

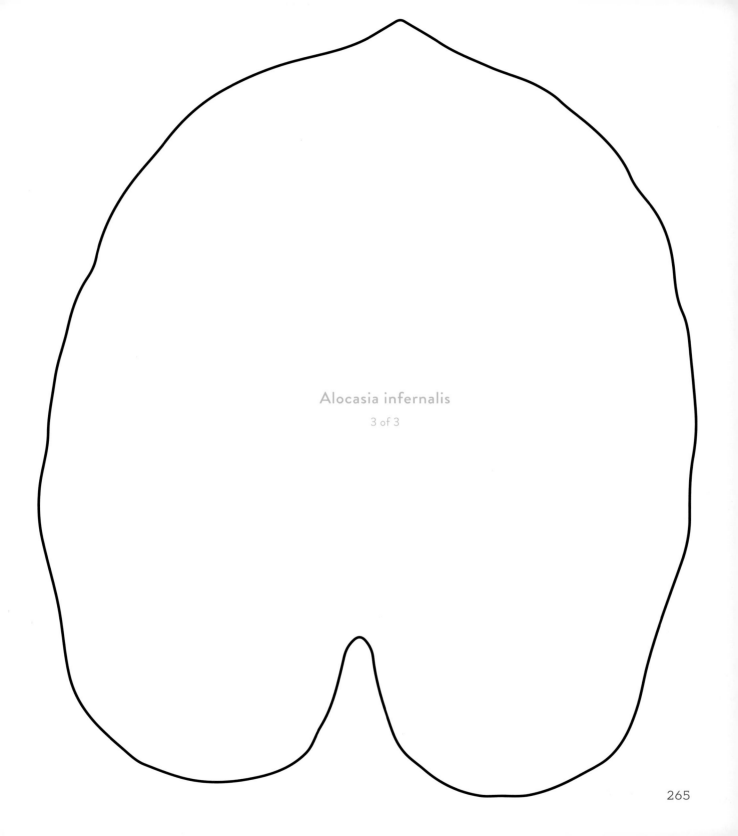

Alocasia infernalis

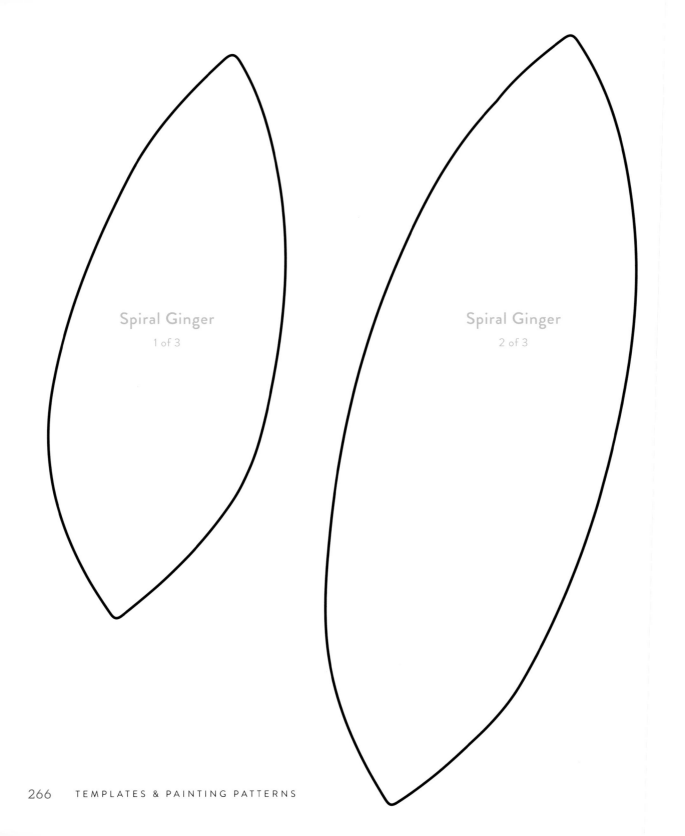

Spiral Ginger

1 of 3

Spiral Ginger

2 of 3

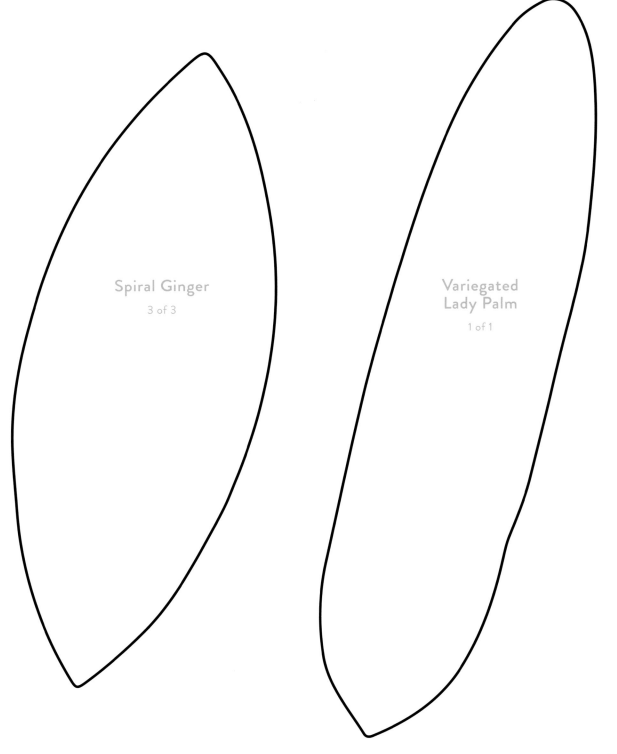

Spiral Ginger

3 of 3

Variegated
Lady Palm

1 of 1

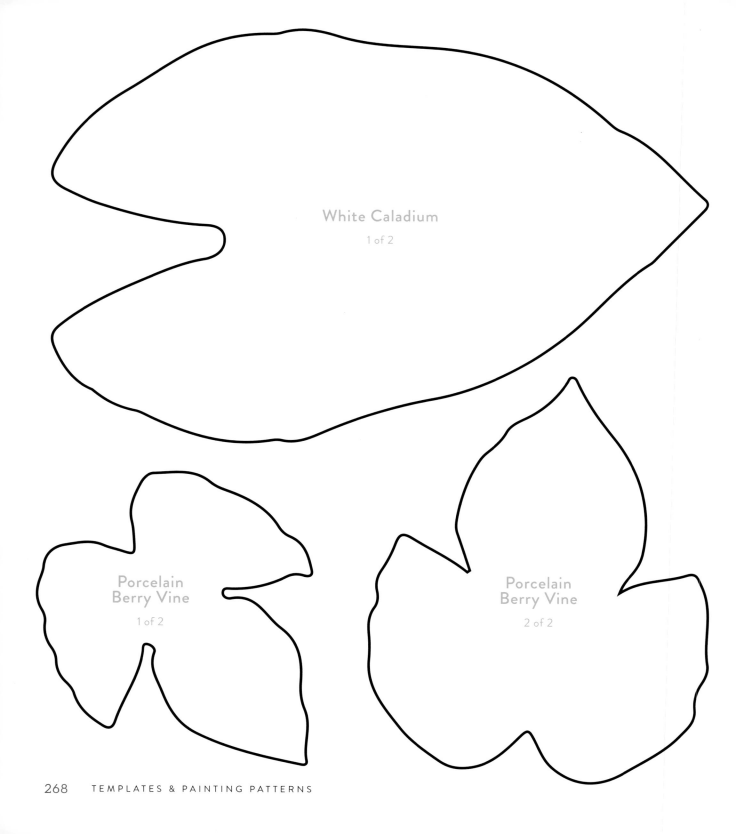

White Caladium

1 of 2

Porcelain
Berry Vine

1 of 2

Porcelain
Berry Vine

2 of 2

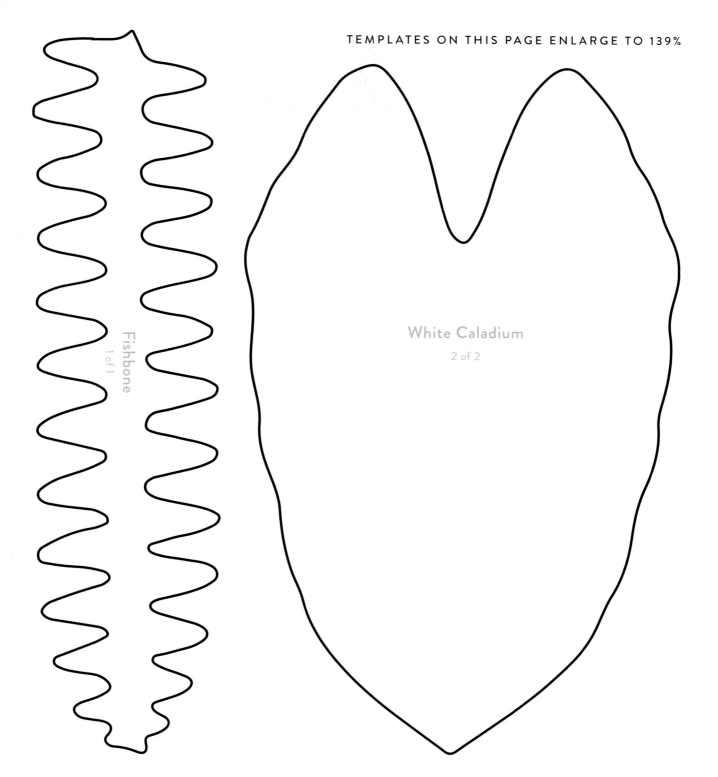

Fishbone

1 of 1

White Caladium

2 of 2

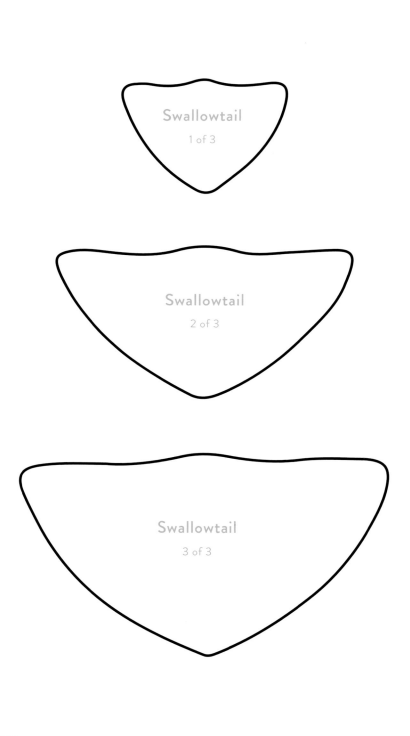

Swallowtail

1 of 3

Swallowtail

2 of 3

Swallowtail

3 of 3

Pink Cordyline

1 of 1

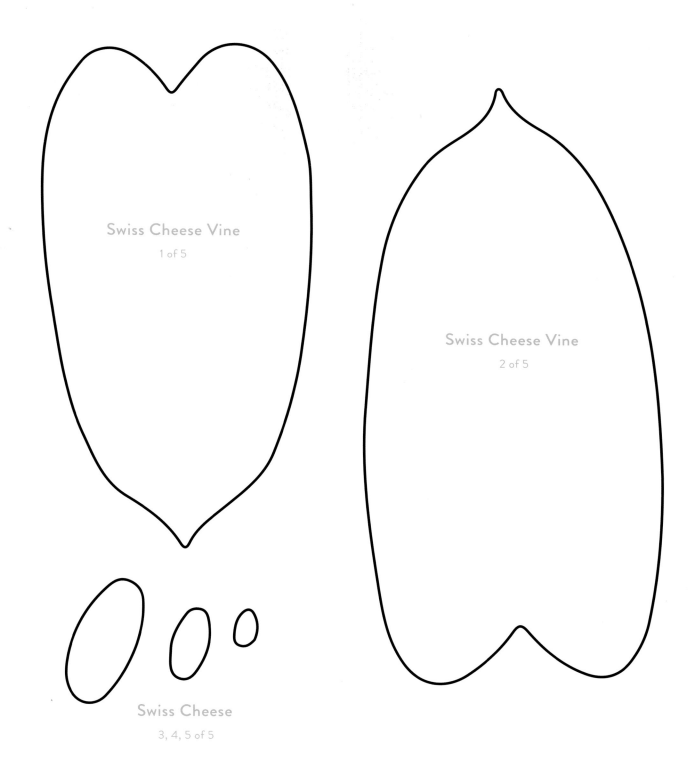

Swiss Cheese Vine

1 of 5

Swiss Cheese Vine

2 of 5

Swiss Cheese

3, 4, 5 of 5

Angel Wing Begonia

1 of 3

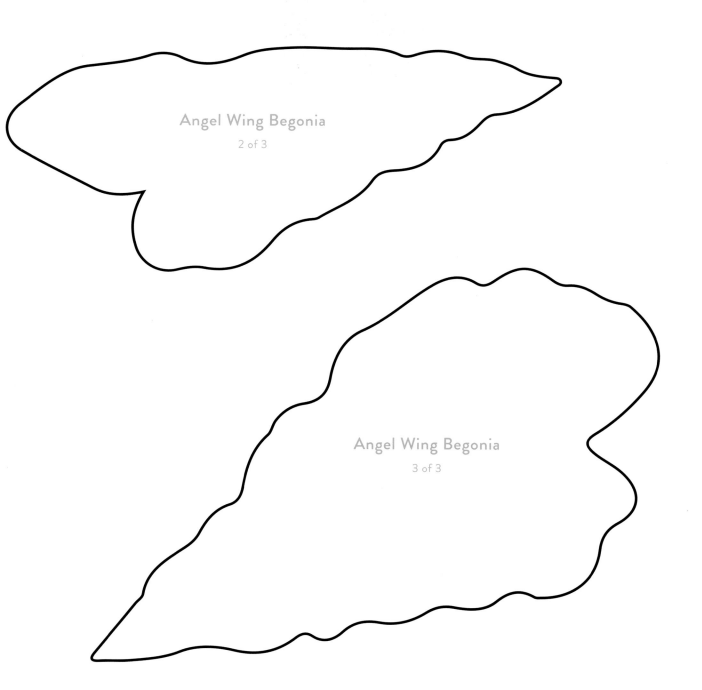

Angel Wing Begonia
2 of 3

Angel Wing Begonia
3 of 3

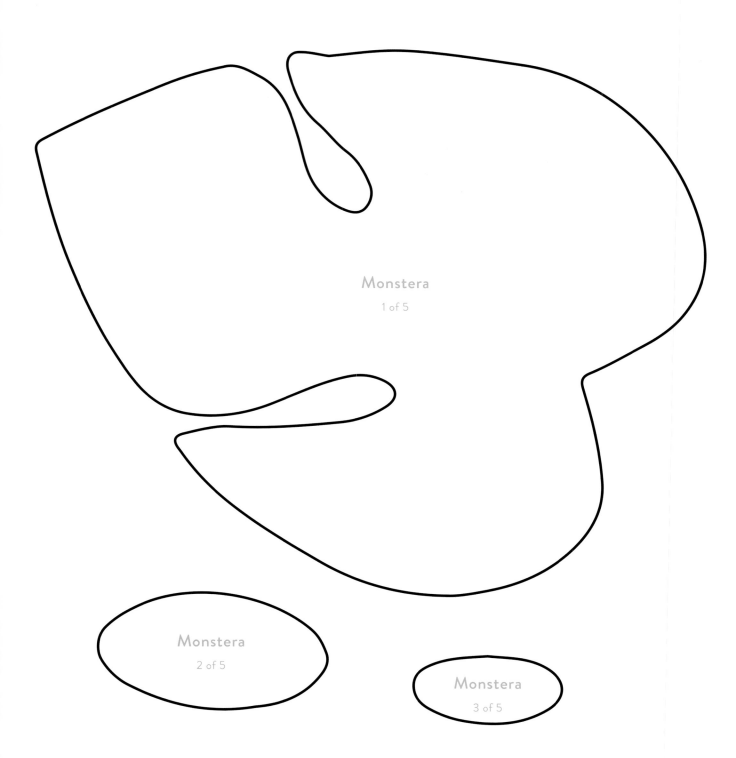

Monstera

1 of 5

Monstera

2 of 5

Monstera

3 of 5

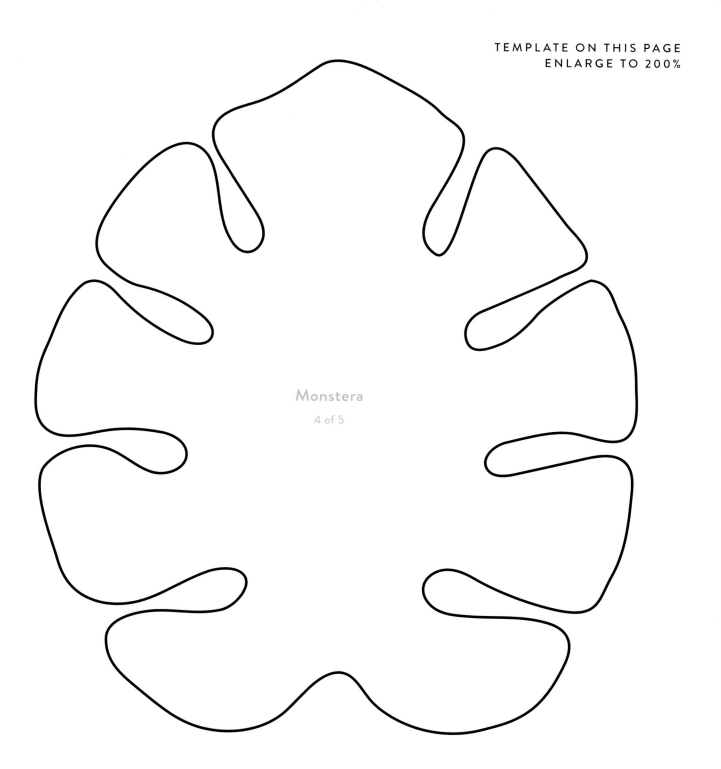

Monstera

4 of 5

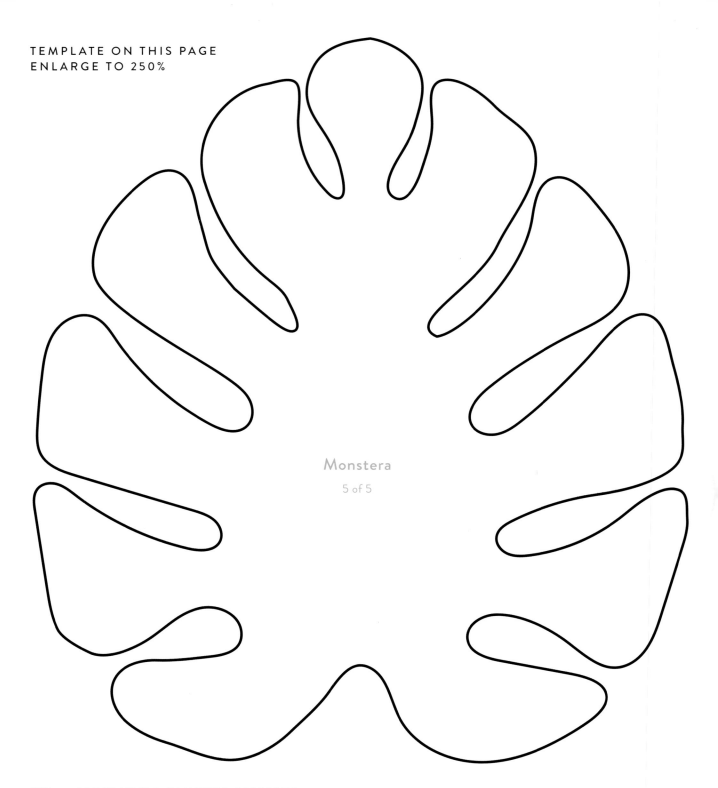

Monstera

5 of 5

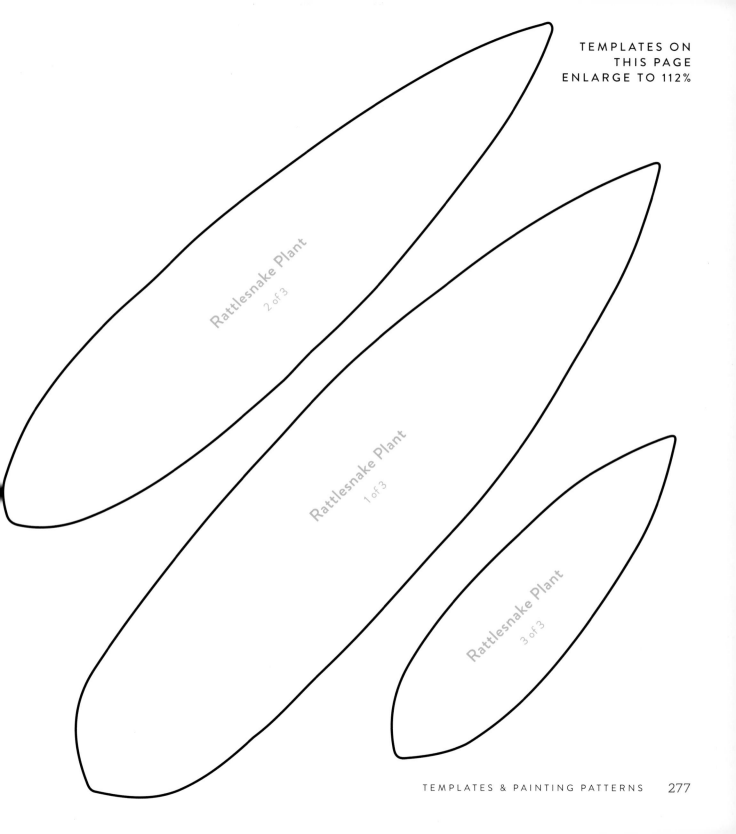

Rattlesnake Plant
2 of 3

Rattlesnake Plant
1 of 3

Rattlesnake Plant
3 of 3

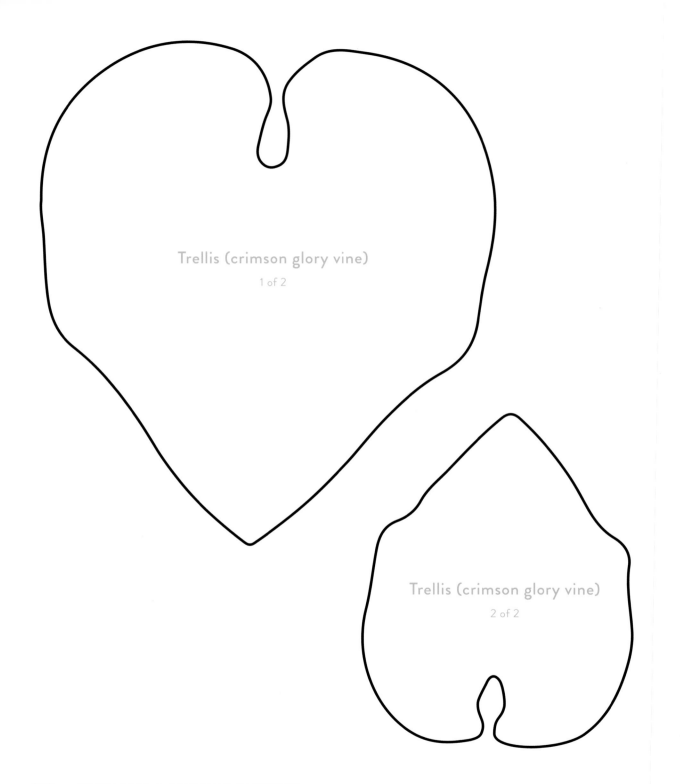

Trellis (crimson glory vine)

1 of 2

Trellis (crimson glory vine)

2 of 2

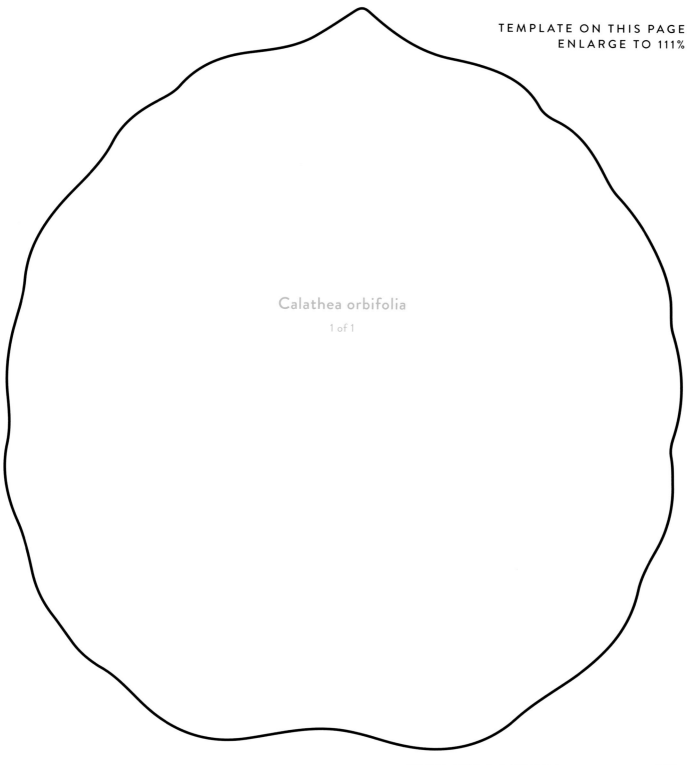

Calathea orbifolia

1 of 1

Tapioca

1 of 2

Tapioca

2 of 2

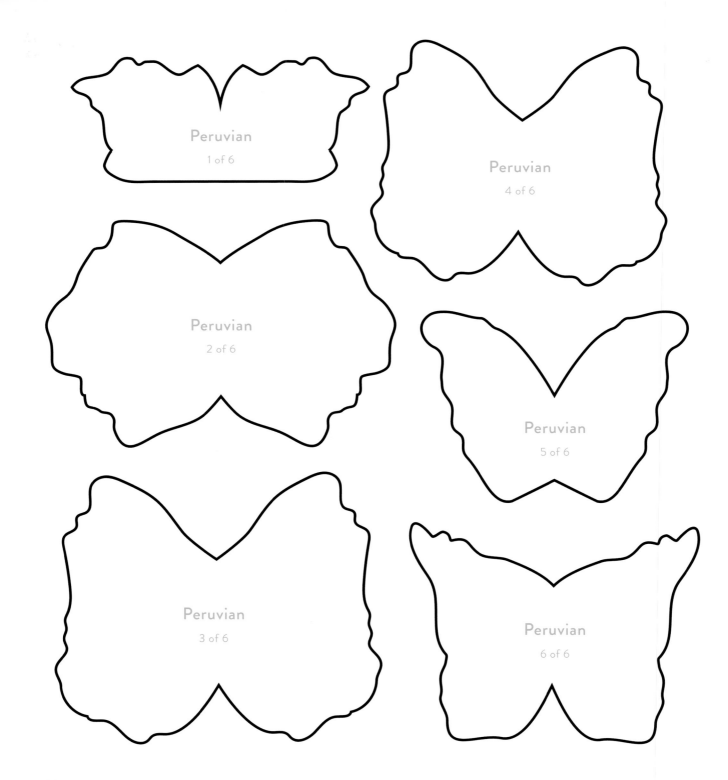

Peruvian
1 of 6

Peruvian
4 of 6

Peruvian
2 of 6

Peruvian
5 of 6

Peruvian
3 of 6

Peruvian
6 of 6

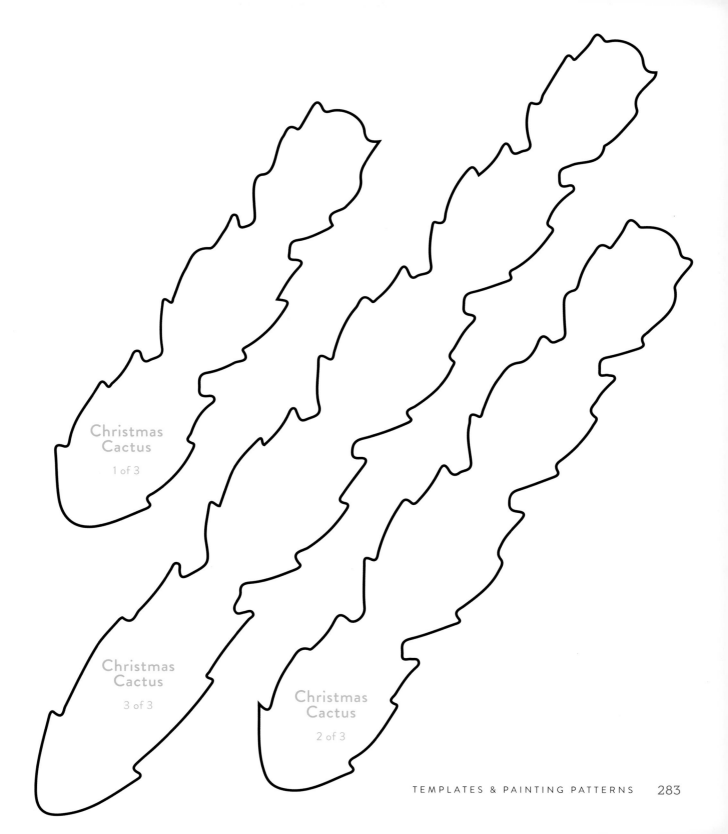

Christmas Cactus

1 of 3

Christmas Cactus

3 of 3

Christmas Cactus

2 of 3

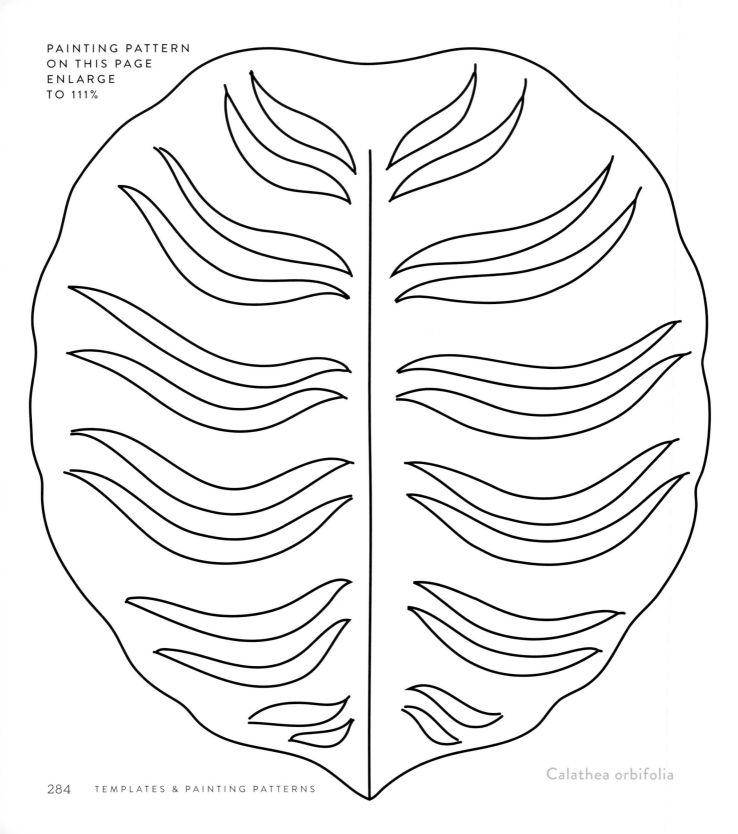

Calathea orbifolia

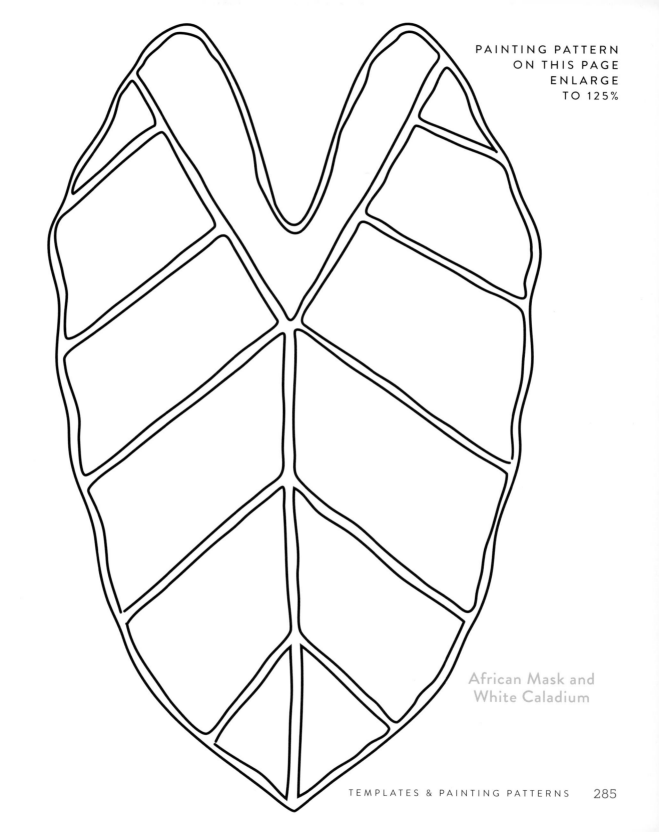

African Mask and
White Caladium

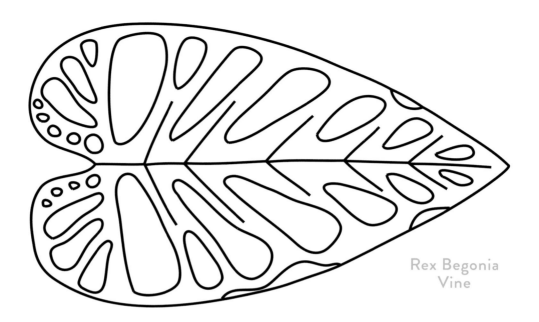

Rex Begonia
Vine

Watermelon
Peperomia

Swallowtail

Rattlesnake
Plant

Resources

STRAIGHT FLORAL WIRE Decora (decora.it) paper-covered floral stem wire, available at amazon.com.

DOUBLE-SIDED ADHESIVE Grafix (grafixarts.com) double tack mounting film, available at jerrysartarama.com, dickblick.com, amazon.com and more.

GENERAL ART AND CRAFT SUPPLIES

Amazon: amazon.com

Dick Blick: dickblick.com

Michael's: michaels.com

Jerry's Artarama: jerrysartarama.com

Artist and Craftsman Supply: artistcraftsman.com

PAPER

Paper Presentation: paperpresentation.com

Paper Source: papersource.com

Staples: staples.com

VESSELS

Anthropologie: anthropologie.com

H and M Home: hm.com

Jamali Garden: jamaligarden.com

Target: target.com

Terrain: shopterrain.com

West Elm: westelm.com

Acknowledgments

First and foremost, thank you, dear readers, this book is for you! I am honored for the opportunity to have made it. This book would not have been possible without the generous patience, guidance, and encouragement from my friends and family. Thank you, Ryan, for your unwavering support and for dealing with months on end of paper plants taking over our apartment. I love you to the moon and back. Thank you, Corey, for lending your endless know-how and wisdom. Thank you, Christine, for your beautiful photos and newfound friendship. I feel so lucky! Thank you, Steph, for your crafting, hauling, and mad-skillz. Thank you, David, for always encouraging and believing in me. Thank you, Alicia, for motivating and advising me early on. You will always be an inspiration to me. Thank you, Alexis, for your friendship and advice from the moment of inception. Thank you to my editor, Lesley Bruynesteyn, for her thorough and thoughtful attention to detail! Thank you, Anne Kenady Smith and Hillary Caudle, who designed this book, and to all my partners at Timber Press. Thank you: Russ, Kristen, James, Audrey, Sarah B., Sarah M., Jodi, Brittany, Aaron, Susie, Gustavo, Jillian, Joey, Lauren, Laura, Aly, Katie, Mary Kate, Allisan, Malinda, Peyton, Matthew, Marilyn, and to all those who have cheered me on, I am forever grateful.

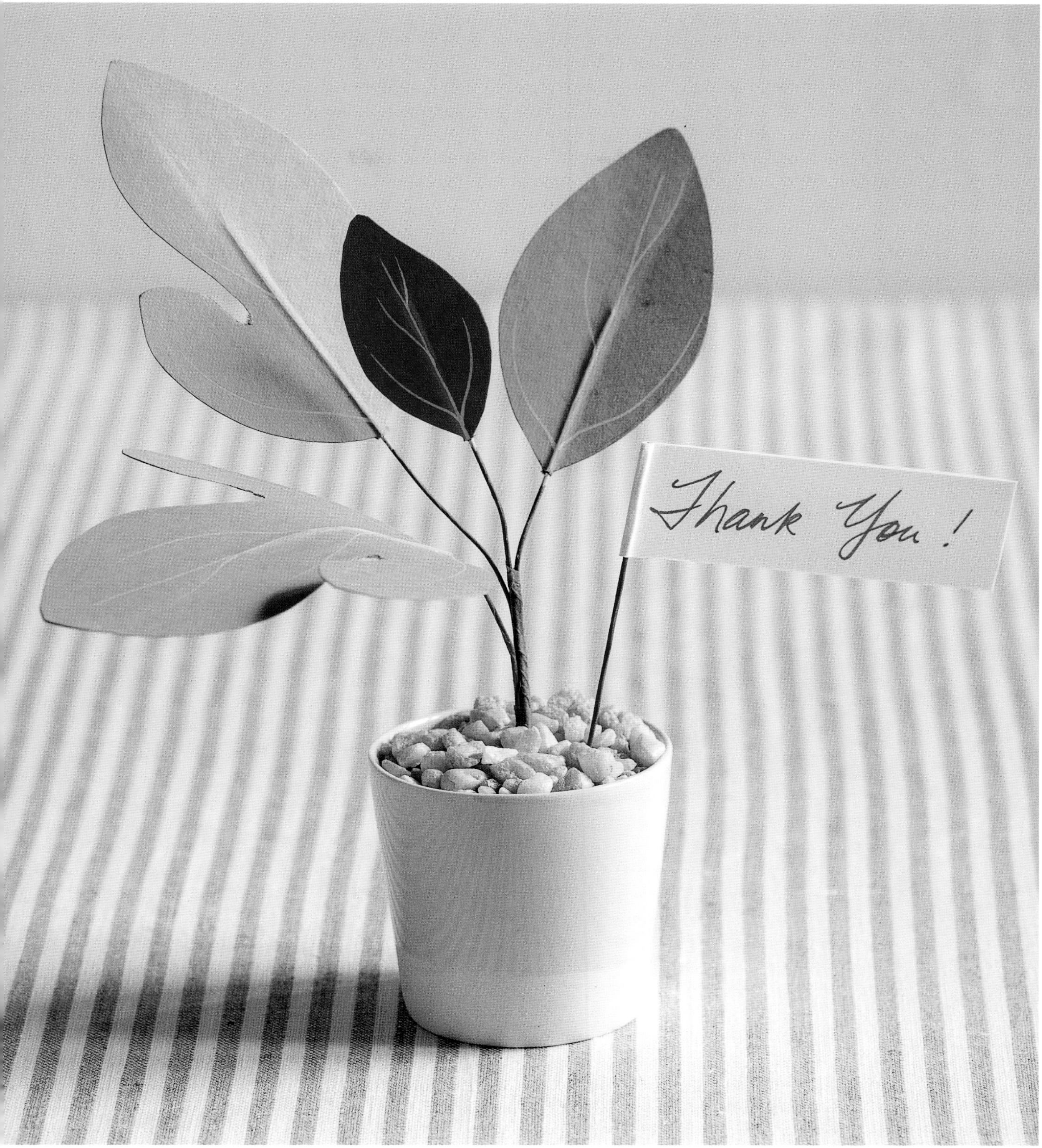
Thank You!

Index

CORRIE BETH HOGG is a lifelong artist. She is the art and craft director for world-renowned event-design company David Stark Design and Production. With David, she has created work seen in *Martha Stewart Living*, *The New York Times*, *Better Homes and Gardens*, *Vogue.com*, *InStyle.com*, *Domino*, and more. An ardent student of nature, Corrie renders her favorite plants in paper with whimsy and careful craftsmanship. Her creations have appeared in *The House That Lars Built*, *Design*Sponge*, *Wallpaper**, and *Gardenista*, among others. Originally from Mississippi, Corrie now calls Brooklyn, New York, home. This is Corrie's first book.

CHRISTINE HAN is a commercial and editorial photographer specializing in food culture, still life, portraits, and lifestyle. Her approach is relaxed and collaborative, and she excels in making natural, authentic imagery. Her commercial clients include Bose, Pepsi, Shake Shack, and Starbucks, and her work has been featured in publications and on blogs such as *Good Housekeeping*, *Food & Wine*, *Apartment Therapy*, and *Food52*, among others. She lives in Brooklyn, New York, and she enjoys traveling and being outdoors. Find her online at christinehanphotography.com.